Photographer's Guide to the Mid-Hudson Valley

Third Edition
2019

Jeffrey David Montanye

Book design by Jeff Montanye
Photographs by Jeff Montanye
Copyright © 2019 by Montanye Arts Publishing
Published by Montanye Arts
www.jeffreydmontanye.com

For information write:
Assistacomp, PO Box 148, Bullville, NY 10915 or call 845-361-2029

ISBN 978-0-9779702-6-1

TABLE OF CONTENTS

Preface

The Hudson Valley is a treasure trove of unique photographic gems. Hudson Valley Photo Guide was founded for the sole purpose of guiding amateur photographers through this photographic world. Not only to lead you to some of the best kept secrets around the Hudson Valley but also to be a guide through your camera and it's technical enigmas. A Photographer's Guide to the Mid-Hudson Valley is your own personal photography training guide with tricks and tips that will help you capture unusual photographs. It is your guide to photographer friendly places where you can take great photographs.

This book is *not* finished. It will never be finished. But that isn't going to stop me from publishing it. I've been criticized for publishing it before having every single park, every corner of the Hudson Valley cataloged but then it may never be finished for the Hudson Valley is a vast resource of wonders and beauty. I know people who have been writing a book for years and they probably will never finish it. So just take from it what you can and maybe the next edition will be the completed one. Perhaps you know of a great location, photographer friendly business, event or public attraction to be included. Feel free to contact me.

Assistacomp is a training/consulting business to help those in need of assistance with technology and software. All classes are designed and taught by Jeff Montanye from Bullville, NY. Classes are held at the Orange-Ulster BOCES adult education program in Goshen, New York as well as libraries in the Ramapo Catskill Library System.

The photography classes are designed for anyone who is interested in learning about their digital camera and how to take great photographs. I have created two levels of classes where anyone can fit in comfortably whether first time, beginner digital camera users to those who want to learn about taking professional photographs.

www.jeffreydmontanye.com

Use this guide along with your camera manual and some maps of the area, grab your camera and go shoot some photos.

WATER FRONT

The Hudson Valley has enchanted people for generations. The beauty and mystery of the Hudson Valley has attracted great explorers from around the world. We are modern day explorers capturing the Hudson Valley with our Digital Cameras much as Washington Irving captured the Hudson Valley with his pen years ago.

Replicas of the great tall ships such as the Half Moon recapture the mystery and wonder of yesteryear when the great explorers such as Henry Hudson first navigated the Hudson River. Today we can retrace their steps and experience the Hudson Valley and all of its wonder while capturing it with our cameras.

The Hudson River, once known to the Mohican Indians as Muhheakantuck ("Great Waters Constantly in Motion"), was the site of key battles in the American Revolution. It also inspired an important phase of landscape painting called the Hudson River school that celebrated the natural beauty of the American landscape. Today, the Hudson is one of the nation's most important waterways. Oceangoing ships can navigate the river to Albany year-round. Pleasure boats and tugboat and barge traffic can reach the Great Lakes from May to November. Cargo such as wood pulp, steel, cocoa beans, grain, and scrap metal rely on the Hudson for deliveries. The U.S. Military Academy at West Point also overlooks the Hudson River.

The Newburgh waterfront is probably the best place in the Mid-Hudson Valley area to see the tall ships docked. If you are lucky enough to be in the area as they sail in and out then you want to be near the Bear Mountain Bridge for some great shots. Watch your local news papers or the websites of the ships to find out when they will be in the area.

Sloop Clearwater on the Hudson River, Bannerman's Castle and Storm King Mountain in background
Canon T3i, f13, 1/500 sec, ISO 400

Long Dock Park, Beacon
Canon 7D, f11, 30 seconds, 26mm, ISO 200

Beacon Waterfront

The Beacon waterfront is home to some wonderful photographic opportunities with Scenic Hudson's Long Dock Park, Pete and Toshi Seeger Riverfront Park, Dennings Point State Park. There's even a waterfall of sorts on Fishkill Creek at Madam Brett Park just a stone's throw from the waterfront. History abounds here going back hundreds of years. Once bustling with industry the waterfront has been transformed into the beautiful parks seen today. From oil terminals, warehouses and junk yards to kayak pavilions, boat launches and parks the waterfront is a far cry from what it used to be. Hike the 1-mile Klara Sauer Trail which spans the waterfront from the Beacon train station to Denning's Point State Park. You can go home with some interesting photos even in the winter.

Croton Point Park

Croton Point Park is a 508-acre park situated on a peninsula just off Route 9 below Peekskill. The park juts into the Hudson River from the east shore and is prominently flat offering views of the river and Hook Mountain to the south. There are facilities for picnicking, camping, hiking and swimming. The park, rich in natural and human history, is also the site of historic wine cellars that are thought of be the oldest in New York State and the Croton Point Nature Center.

Croton Point Park, Croton, NY
Canon 7D, f14, 1/25 sec, 55mm, ISO 100, EV-0.3

Dockside Park, Cold Spring, Putnam County

This park, although small in acreage, is one of the most spectacular places to photograph the Hudson River Valley. It offers breathtaking views of Breakneck Ridge to the north, West Point to the south, and Storm King Mountain across the river to the west. The region, known as the Hudson Highlands and appropriately named the Northern Gate of the Hudson Valley is a favorite area of both photographers and painters. In this area, mountains on either bank of the river narrow to form an entryway to the wider section South of that point.

Hudson River Parks:

Along the Hudson River are many parks that provide up close views and access to the river. If you want to be so close that you can touch the water, these parks will get you there.

Location	Town	County	Page
Black Creek Preserve	Esopus	Uster County	
Charles Rider	Kingston	Uster County	
Croton Point Park	Croton	Westchester County	5
Dennings Point	Beacon	Dutchess County	
Dockside Park	Cold Spring	Putnam County	6
Esopus Meadows Preserve	Glasco	Ulster County	
Foundry Dock Park	Cold Spring	Putnam County	
Highland Landing Park	Highland	Ulster County	
Kaal Rock Park	Poughkeepsie	Dutchess County	
Lighthouse Park	Esopus	Ulster County	
Long Dock Park	Beacon	Dutchess County	4
Newburgh Waterfront www.newburghonhudson.com	Newburgh	Orange County	2
Plum Point	Newburgh	Orange County	
Quiet Cove Riverfront Park	Poughkeepsie	Dutchess County	
Robert E Post Memorial Park	Kingston	Ulster County	
Sleightsburgh Park	Esopus	Ulster County	
Stony Point Battlefield	Stony Point	Rockland County	
Waryas Park	Poughkeepsie	Dutchess County	

Exposure

The first thing you need to know about photography is exposure. Inside your camera is a light sensitive device. This used to be film but today's modern cameras use an electronic device called a Charged Coupled Device or CCD chip. Light goes through the lens of the camera which magnifies it and focuses it onto the CCD chip. The chip becomes "exposed" once light hits it as film used to. When the chip is exposed it collects the information and sends it to the camera's computer processor to produce the photograph. Like film, the exposure has to be just right or the photograph will be too light or too dark. There are three ways to control the exposure:

1) Aperture
2) Shutter Speed
3) ISO

This is known as the exposure triangle. When your camera is in automatic mode it will decide the correct settings for you. When you press the shutter release button, the camera's light meter reads the light coming into the lens and calculates which aperture, shutter speed and ISO settings to use for the best exposure. This works good for snapshots but there is a lot more to proper exposure than what the camera can do automatically.

Aperture and Shutter Speed

Exposing a photograph is much like filling a glass up with water. The camera fills the picture up with light the same way your faucet fills the glass with water. A perfect exposure is when the glass is filled to the top. There is no water running over and no air in the glass at all.

When you turn the spigot on your faucet, water begins to flow out the end and into your glass. As you turn the spigot a small hole or orifice inside the pipes opens up. This hole gets larger as you turn the knob allowing more water to flow. The orifice is like the aperture in your camera's lens. As you open the aperture more light "pours" into the camera.

You can control how much water flows by how much you open the spigot. But you have to limit how long the water is flowing. At some point, you must turn the spigot back off or the water will over flow out of the glass. This is equivalent to shutter speed. Shutter speed controls how long the light pours into the camera. Too long and the photo is over exposed. Too short and the photo is under exposed.

If you open the spigot just a little bit, you must hold the glass under the faucet much longer to fill it. If you open the spigot up full blast you need to shut it down quickly or the glass will overflow. The same thing applies to photography. If you open the aperture just a little bit you have to keep the shutter open longer to get a good exposure and vise versa.

Sensitivity to Light

Sometimes the well doesn't have much water in it and our faucet can't flow fast even with the spigot all the way open. Now you have no choice but to hold the glass under the faucet for a long time. The same thing happens with light. If there is little light on your subject even large apertures cannot prevent the need for long exposures.

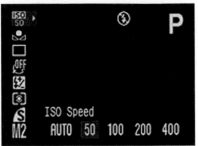

One solution is to turn on your flash. In automatic mode, your camera will do this for you. When you turn on flash it's like someone is standing next to you with a pitcher of water and quickly fills your glass with water from the pitcher.

Another solution is to make the CCD chip inside your camera more sensitive to light. To do this you need to adjust the ISO setting. The ISO adjustment can be made from your camera's menu system or a button on the camera itself. By adjusting the ISO setting you are making the CCD chip more sensitive or less sensitive to light.

Looking back at our water faucet analogy, imagine that we switched the glass with a smaller glass. It won't take as long to fill up with water if the glass is smaller. The ISO setting in your camera changes the sensitivity of the CCD chip. So we can say that changing the ISO is like changing the size of the glass. It's important to note that larger ISO numbers are more sensitive to light than small numbers. ISO 400 is half the size of ISO 200 when comparing it to the glass of water.

Automatic Exposure

Your camera will set the exposure for you automatically. It will decide the best aperture, shutter speed, ISO and use of flash on it's own without you touching anything. However, shutter speed, aperture and ISO will drastically effect your photos depending on the values that are chosen. This is where automatic mode fails us. Your camera has no way to determine which values to set, only that the settings need to be set in such a way that the photograph is not too dark or too light. Therein lies the first problem. How does the camera know if you want the shot to be dark or bright. It doesn't. So it guesses. What about depth of field? Will the camera choose a small aperture with a long shutter speed or a large aperture with a short shutter speed? Automatic mode is based on typical, average behavior and assumptions. If your photography goes beyond typical and average then automatic mode is not for you! To improve your photography you must understand how shutter speed, aperture and ISO settings work together.

Exposure Stops

As mentioned earlier, there are three ways to control exposure: aperture, shutter speed and ISO. If any one of the three changes, one or both of the other two must change to compensate and keep the same exposure. It's a simple mathematical formula. Imagine a triangle with a four at each corner.

4 x 4 x 4

If you double one of the corners, to keep the formula the same, you must halve one of the other corners.

8 x 2 x 4
8 x 4 x 2

If you double one corner twice you can halve the other two.

2 x 16 x 2

In each example the product is the same: 64. We just got there in different ways. However, photography doesn't use simple numbers like this. Cameras have seconds or fractions of a second for shutter speeds, ISO for sensitivity and f-stops for apertures. But how do we convert all of this into easy numbers to calculate in our heads? The answer is stops. Exposure is measured in stops. Each stop is double or half the exposure. Another way of putting it is double or half the amount of light. For example, if I increase my shutter speed from 1/60 of a second to 1/30 of a second I doubled the length of time the shutter will be open. Double the length of time means double the light. I increased the exposure one stop. Aperture and ISO both have exposure stops as well.

> Changing exposure settings is like keeping a scale in balance. On one side you have a properly exposed image. On the other side you have aperture, shutter speed and ISO. If you take away some aperture the scale tips. You must add shutter speed or ISO to keep the balance. It's the same for each setting.

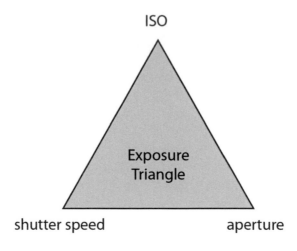

ISO

Exposure
Triangle

shutter speed   aperture

Shutter Speed Values

The shutter is a closed curtain that sits between the lens and the light sensitive chip inside the camera (CCD). Like film, the CCD chip is always sensitive to light and must be kept in the dark. This curtain blocks the light from exposing the chip inside your camera. When you take a photo the curtain moves out of the way. It's released. Which is why the button you press to take a photo is called the shutter release. The curtain stays out of the way for a programmed amount of time. This is the shutter speed. The longer the shutter is open the more light is allowed in. The exposure can be increased or decreased by slowing down and speeding up the shutter speed. Slowing down the shutter increases the exposure. Speeding up the shutter decreases the exposure. When the shutter speed is doubled, the exposure is decreased one stop. When the shutter speed is cut in half, the exposure is increased one stop. It's all about time. Light adds up with time.

Shutter speed is probably the easiest part of the exposure triangle to understand. Fast shutter speeds freeze motion. Slow shutter speeds blur motion. How fast or slow the shutter needs to be depends on how fast the subject is moving and how much blur you want to capture.

Older cameras had shutter speeds with values that double or halve with each change: 1/15, 1/30, 1/60, 1/125, 1/250. Each click of the dial was a full stop. This made calculating in your head easy. Today's modern cameras have more settings in between. Usually one third stops. This gives us many more shutter speeds to choose from. It's good that the camera can do the math for us but it is important to understand what is happening even if you don't ever want to do the math in your head.

The range of your camera's shutter speeds depends on the make and model of the camera body. Most cameras range between 1/5000 of a second to 30 seconds.

1/3 second   1/20 second   1/2000 second

Your camera will show you on the view screen what shutter speed is being selected. Sometimes your camera will leave off the numerator (1) and will only display the denominator (250). Don't get confused and think this is 250 seconds. If your camera's shutter speed goes beyond fractions, seconds are denoted by double tick marks ("). A five second shutter speed will be displayed as 5". A one fifth shutter speed will

be displayed as 5. A half second is displayed as 0"5.

Showing Motion

There are two ways to capture and show motion in your photographs. The first is to use a fast shutter speed to freeze motion as shown in the second image below. This technique works best when objects are flying in the air such as a soccer ball being kicked. Another way is to allow portions of the image to blur. A slow shutter speed will blur motion. Review the two waterfall photos below. The camera can't know what the photographer's needs are. You'll have to take control and choose the shutter speed manually.

f22, 1/6 sec, ISO 100

f5, 1/200 sec, ISO 100

Panning

A technique called panning is used to capture motion when the subject is moving parallel to the camera. The photographer follows the subject through the view finder and snaps the shot while the camera is moving along with the subject. From the camera's point of view, the subject isn't moving, the background is. Using a fairly slow shutter speed of about 1/30th of a second will blur the background giving the appearance that the subject is moving fast.

Goshen Historic Track
Canon 7D, 70mm, 1/30 @ f16, ISO 100, color saturation +2

Aperture Values

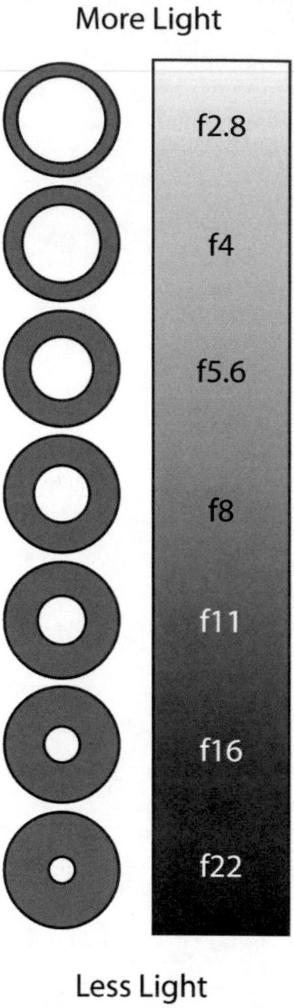

The way aperture settings effect your photos isn't as forth-coming as shutter speed is. Shutter speed controls blur caused by motion. Aperture also affects image blur but in the form of focus or sharpness.

Aperture settings are measured in f-stops. How an f-stop is calculated is beyond what most photographers care to under-stand and those who don't understand it take just as nice a picture as those who do. It's actually a ratio between the diameter of the aperture of the lens and the distance from the CCD chip in the camera. What is important to under-stand is that it's a fraction. Therefore the smaller numbers refer to larger aperture openings and the larger numbers refer to smaller aperture openings. When one announces that they are using a large aperture this is not a reference to the number dialed in on the lens, rather the size of the actual hole inside the lens. This means that f2.8 is a larger aperture whereas f22 is a smaller aperture.

As a photographer your concerns lie in what constitutes as a full stop so you can easily adapt it with your shutter speed and ISO settings. The primary concern being the area of the aperture itself. If the area is doubled, twice the light is al-lowed to expose the CCD chip. If the area is halved then half the light is allowed to expose the chip. The chart on the right shows the most common f-stops in full stop increments.

Of coarse, most digital cameras by default adjust the aper-ture by 1/3 stop increments as you click the command dial back and forth. You'll have to remember that as you make your adjustments. But that is a lot to memorize so most of us know the standard full stop increments as listed here.

More Light

f2.8

f4

f5.6

f8

f11

f16

f22

Less Light

The Aperture is located in the lens, not the camera body which means the aperture range will vary depending on the lens you are using. Older cameras had apertures with values that double or halve with each change: f2.8, f4, f5.6, etc. Each change was one complete stop making calculating in your head easy. Today's modern cameras have more settings in between. Usually one third stops. This gives us many more f-stops to choose from but if you want to increase or decrease the aperture by one stop you'll have to move the dial 3 clicks. Once again, because of the many options, having the camera do our calculations make it easier but it is important to understand what is happening even if you don't ever want to do the math in your head.

With all this confusion, why do we even care what aperture we use? Because the beneficial and adverse effects on your photographs are immense.

Depth of Field

Perhaps the most obvious effect aperture has on your photography is Depth of Field. The point of focus refers to the exact point that you focused your camera on. Depth of field refers to how much is in focus in front of and behind the point of focus. Large aperture settings (small numbers) will give you a short depth of field. In other words, very little will be in focus in front of and behind your focus point. Small apertures (large numbers) will give you a large depth of field. Refer to the top two images on the next page.

So if you want to have beautifully blurred backgrounds you'll need to open your aperture large but if you want sharp landscapes you'll have to close the aperture down. Of course changing aperture values means changing shutter speed and ISO appropriately to keep the exposure correct. Using Aperture Priority mode will handle this automatically.

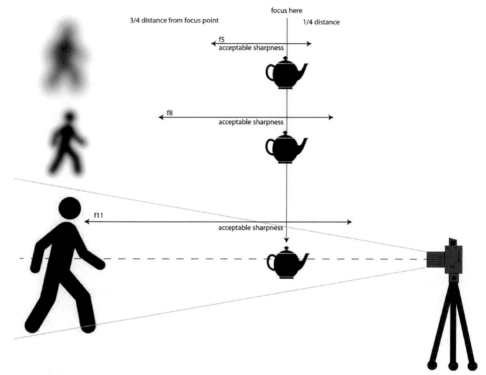

Depth of field preview

When looking through the view finder to compose your shot the aperture is always wide open no matter what it is set to. This makes sure there is plenty of light to see the subject clearly in the view finder. As soon as you press the shutter release the aperture closes down to the value it is set to just before the image is recorded. So when viewing the image through the view finder you will see a short depth of field all the time no matter what aperture you select. Some cameras have a depth of field preview button usually located on the camera body close to the bottom side of the lens. When you press this button the aperture will close down to the actual value it is set to as you are looking through the view finder. The problem is that a small aperture lets less light in so the image in the view finder will be dark. You will notice though, that foreground and background objects look more in focus just as the final recorded image will look. See bottom of page 21.

f5.0, 1/60sec, ISO 400   *f29, 1/30 sec, ISO 6400*

Depth of Field vs Focal length

There are two ways to increase magnification of your subject in the view finder of your camera. First, you can change the distance between the camera and the subject by walking closer. Second, you can change the focal length of the lens by zooming or changing lenses. Focal length is the distance between the lens and the image sensor when the subject is in focus. Have you noticed when you zoom in with a zoom lens to increase the magnification of your subject in the view finder, the lens extrudes more from the camera? This happens because you are changing the focal length of the lens. Both methods of increasing magnification effect depth of field in the same way. The greater the magnification, the smaller the depth of field. Some people will tell you that a telephoto lens has a smaller depth of field than a standard or wide angle lens. This is both correct *and* incorrect. It really depends on how you look at it. If you setup two cameras side by side, one with a telephoto lens and one with a standard or wide angle lens and viewed the same subject in the view finder it will appear that the telephoto lens has a much smaller depth of field than the other lens. And you will be correct, the depth of field will be smaller. However, you wouldn't be looking at the exact same image. The image in the view finder of the camera with the telephoto lens will be magnified where the image in the other camera will not. Therefore, to make a true comparison you will have to move the camera with the standard or wide angle lens closer to the subject so that the image in the view finder will appear exactly the same as the image in the other camera. When you do that, the depth of field will decrease as you move closer until it matches the camera with the telephoto lens. Therefore the two lenses will have the same depth of field.

Forced perspective

How do you take your best friend and cram her inside a tiny little teapot? Movies such as *Honey I Shrunk the Kids* and *Lord of the Rings* use the same basic methods you see here to make people appear small. It's all in aperture and focus settings as well as strategically placed subjects.

To make people appear smaller you will have to position them far in the background of the photo. The further away, the smaller they appear. We'll call this the *far* subject. Objects you want to appear larger will be placed up close to the camera. We'll call this the *close* subject.

For camera settings, you will need a very small aperture such as f22 or smaller if your lens allows it. You will have to place your camera in aperture priority mode to achieve this. It's best to use a tripod but you may have to turn up your ISO setting to speed up your shutter speed. This way you won't get motion blur if your subject moves a little. Remember what we learned about depth of field? The closer you are to your subject, the smaller the depth of field is. So you don't want to focus on the far or close subjects. Instead, focus between them. To get the largest possible depth of field between the far and close subjects you will need to focus 1/4 the distance between them. To do this you will have to use manual focus. You can temporarily have someone stand in this area, get your focus, then have them move out of the way. This will place the far subject at the furthest reach of focus and the close subject at the closest reach of focus. See the figure below. Unfortunately, focus isn't the same sharpness throughout the entire depth of field. Focus is sharpest at the exact point of focus and gets softer toward the far reaches of the depth of field. Placing your subjects at the far reaches of the depth of field may cause them to be a little soft but acceptable. We call this the *acceptable* sharpness range.

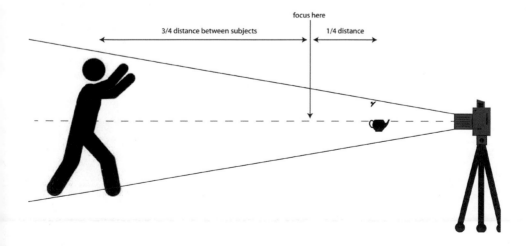

focus here

3/4 distance between subjects   1/4 distance

To the right is a pair of model cars from the 1930's era. We didn't have real cars so we placed models on a board in front of the old police station in Middletown. Using the techniques mentioned on the previous page we were able to take the shot making it look as if there are real cars parked in front of the building.

Below is another technique that doesn't use depth of field. Instead we used a technique called cropping to make the tree appear much larger than it is. By not showing the right side of the tree the brain has no way of telling where the edge of the tree is so it appears to be much larger than it is. These large trees are growing near the Bashakill in Wurtsboro.

Diffraction

As light passes through the iris in a lens some strange things happen. The light bends. This is known as diffraction. If you shine a light on an object in a perfectly dark room it will cast a shadow. If light travels in a straight line, then why isn't the edge of the shadow sharp? Why is it fuzzy? That's because light bends around objects that it hits. When light travels through the iris of a camera it hits the edges of the aperture and bends. The smaller the hole, the more the light bends. This has two unique side effects. The first is that the image will be slightly fuzzy. It loses its over-all sharpness. It also creates a star burst effect around lights. If you can live with a slightly softer image, the star burst effect can be very appealing in your photo.

Below are examples of three different aperture settings. The diagram shows light entering your lens, passing through the aperture and hitting the light sensitive CCD. The images below the diagram show the star burst effect due to diffraction. The bottom row of images show a cropped area from the image above it of a sign on one of the buildings. The sharpness of the image can be seen in this cropped and enlarged section.

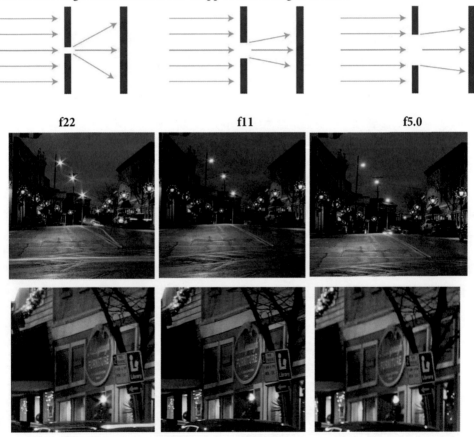

You would think by looking at the top diagrams that as the aperture grew larger the picture would become sharper. But there is another limitation that our lenses suffer from: Spherical Aberrations.

Spherical Aberrations

For the sharpest image, light must be focused to a very fine point. The finer this point, the sharper the image. But how fine can this point be? That depends on the quality of the lens. The problem is that the rate light bends as it passes through a lens at different angles is not a constant. The greater the angle between the light ray and the lens surface at the entry point, the greater the change of angle as it passes through the glass. This means that the rays of light that pass through the lens at its outer edge bend more than the light that enters in through the center. Yes, we expect this to happen but look at the diagram to see what I mean. The light rays towards the outside edges are bending too much so that they are not all meeting at one fine point. This makes the sharp tip of the cone of light dull. It's like drawing with a dull pencil. No matter how hard you try, you can't draw a sharp image with a dull pencil. This is known as spherical aberration. No matter how much you try, you cannot focus down to the smallest point at the tip of the cone.

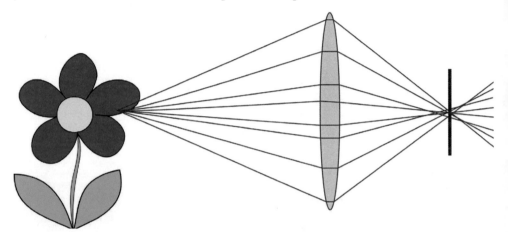

There are ways lens manufacturers can design lenses that will minimize spherical aber-rations but this brings the cost of the lens up. If your lens is not creating sharp images it could mean that it is suffering from severe spherical aberrations. One way to minimize this ill effect is to avoid using large aperture settings. By closing down the aperture you are reducing the spread of wayward light.

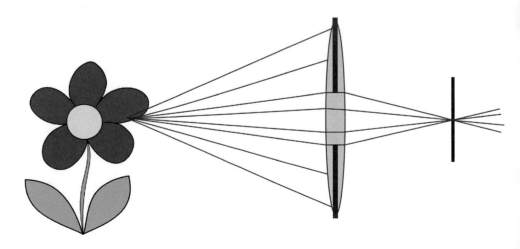

Sweet Spot

If you play tennis you know how important the sweet spot is. It's equally important in a photographic lens. Looking at the images on the bottom of page 19 you can see that a lens loses its sharpness as the aperture gets closer to fully open due to Spherical Aberrations. It also loses its sharpness as the aperture gets closer to its smallest capability due to diffraction. So what is the best aperture to use then? For the sake of obtaining the sharpest image, the best aperture

is usually about two stops down from it's largest capability. This is knows as the lens' sweet spot. With that said I will add that obtaining the sharpest image is not always the most important goal. Sometimes a soft image is more desirable. Often portraits are purposely made soft for effect. A hazy landscape can be more pleasing when softened than when stone sharp. So don't be afraid to use your lens to its maximum aperture options. Just be aware of what is happening.

Lens Speed

The largest aperture a lens can obtain is marked on the lens in the form of a ratio 1:2.8, etc. The maximum aperture on certain zoom lenses varies depending on the focal distance the zoom is set to. Zoom in all the way and the maximum aperture actually gets smaller. These lenses indicate the maximum aperture *range* such as 1:3.5-5.8. Higher quality zoom lenses often keep the same maximum aperture throughout its entire range.

Depth of Field Preview Button

This button closes down the aperture to the value set in the camera controls. It allows the photographer to see the sharpness of the image before the photo is taken. You will notice that the image gets dark when the button is pushed. This is because the aperture is closing down, letting less light in. Not all cameras are equipped with this option.

ISO Values

The acronym has nothing to do with what it actually is. It is the name of the organization that standardizes measurements. ISO stands for International Organization for Standardization. It refers to the sensitivity of emulsion based film. 100 ISO having low sensitivity to light and higher numbers such as 3200 having high sensitivity. This same method of rating has been carried over to modern digital cameras. The most important thing to understand is that when the ISO doubles, the sensitivity to light doubles and when it halves, it's sensitivity halves. ISO settings usually start from 100 and double each step: 100, 200, 400, 800, 1600, 3200, etc.

Exposure Triangle

Now that you have a basic understanding of how each of the exposure settings behave, lets look at our triangle again. In one corner is ISO. You can double or halve this number which will double or halve your camera's sensitivity to light thus doubling or halving the amount of light needed. In the next corner is aperture. Remember, in our simple model each stop doubles or halves the light. In the final corner is shutter speed. Once again, in our simple model each change doubles or halves the speed which doubles or halves the amount of light.

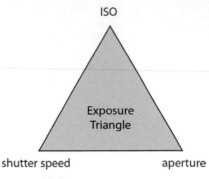

Lets set our camera to ISO 400, f8 and 1/30 shutter speed:

400 x f8 x 1/30

If we double the ISO we need to halve either aperture or shutter speed:

800 x f11 x 1/30
800 x f8 x 1/60

If we double the shutter speed twice, we can halve both the ISO and aperture:

200 x f11 x 1/250

The camera calculates these values for us automatically but as you can see in these examples, there are many different ways to get the same results. Now you have to ask yourself, is there a time when it is beneficial to have a large aperture and fast shutter speed rather than a small aperture and a slow shutter speed; or a high ISO and both a fast shutter speed and small aperture? The answer is YES! The question is When?

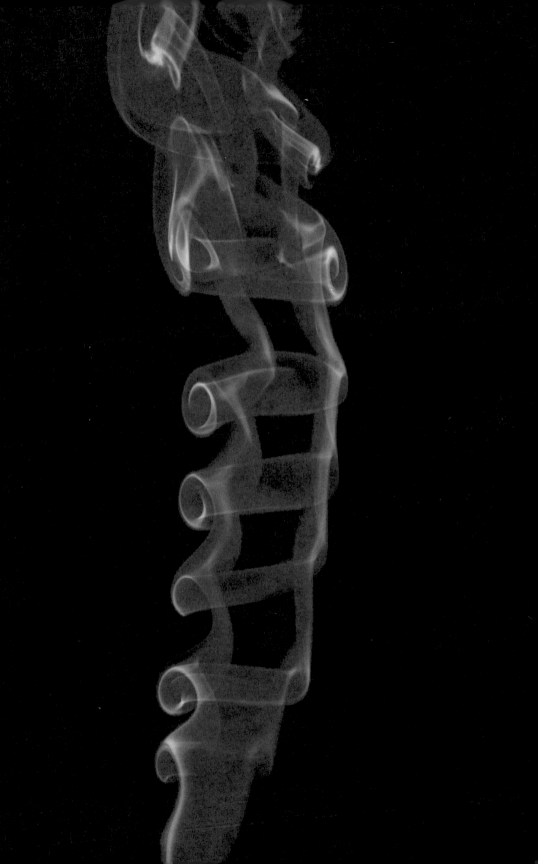

Camera Modes
The camera's mode dial gives us several different ways to
control how the exposure settings are selected.

AUTO In full automatic mode the camera adjusts
aperture, shutter speed and ISO based on aver-
age, typical behavior. You will have no control over what settings are selected. It is best used for quick snapshots where
quality is not important.

Preset Scenes: In automatic mode the camera cannot make
an accurate exposure adjustment because it does not have the ability to understand what
you are photographing. This is your chance to tell the camera what you are photographing.
In these modes the camera is still fully automatic but now that it has more information of
what you are photographing it can calculate a more accurate set of exposure settings.

The original base scene modes are portrait, action, close-up and distance.
Many compact digital cameras have dozens of other scene settings to choose
from in the menu. Selecting one of these modes will help the camera decide
how to adjust aperture, shutter speed and ISO. Each scene lends itself to it's
own exposure settings. Action will favor fast shutter speeds. Portrait and
close-up will favor large apertures. Distance will favor small apertures. Be
forewarned that these modes will also adjust other camera settings such flash
and focus.

These settings help, but the camera takes into consideration that you will be
hand-holding the camera. This means that the shutter speed will be prevented
from going below 1/60th of a second. If slow shutter speeds are desired you
should avoid using these automatic settings.

If you use these preset scenes be certain to read your manual so you understand what each
scene does. I have had people ask me why all of their photos of the kids playing soccer
came out blurry when they used the action mode. It turned out that the game was in the
evening as the sun was going down. Action mode turns flash off. There was not enough
light to achieve fast shutter speeds so all the images had motion blur.

P **Program Mode.** In program mode the camera still works as fully automatic but you
can change the rules. You are given full control of all the camera's settings and the
camera will calculate the three exposure settings automatically around the other
camera settings that you choose. On most cameras you can use the command wheel at
your thumb or index finger to vary the balance of exposure between aperture and shutter speed. Move the wheel in one direction and the shutter speeds increases, reducing
the amount of light exposing the CCD. At the same time the aperture values get larger to
increase the amount of light thus keeping a balance of light and maintaining a correct exposure. Move the wheel in the other direction and the shutter speeds decrease, increasing
light while the aperture decreases, reducing light. As you adjust the command dial each
setting, aperture and shutter speed will shift in opposite directions to keep the exposure in
balance.

A **Aperture Priority (Av):** In this mode, you manually select which aperture you want to use and the camera will automatically choose a shutter speed to balance the exposure. This is sort of a half manual mode. You are manually controlling one aspect of the exposure settings.

S **Shutter Priority (Tv):** In this mode, you select which shutter speed you want to use and the camera will automatically choose an aperture to balance the exposure.
You should realize that the range of shutter speeds is far greater than the range of aperture settings. The chance of selecting a shutter speed that is outside the balance range of aperture settings is high. If you select a very fast or very slow shutter speed there may not be a compatible aperture to keep the exposure in balance. If this happens you will get a very under or over exposed image. Some cameras have a safe guard that will prevent this from happing and may automatically adjust the shutter speed to the closest match or your camera may simply refuse to take the picture. The camera will warn you in some manner such as a blinking shutter speed readout.

M **Manual:** In full manual mode you have control over both the shutter speed and aperture. You can do what every you want with them and the camera will not complain. It is up to you to adjust them properly to get the correct exposure. In this mode the exposure compensation scale acts as a light meter. When the indicator is at zero the exposure is nominal.

Museum Village, Monroe
Canon 7D, 18mm, 1/2sec @ f3.5, ISO 100 EV-1

A fantastic place to find great photography opportunities is in the abundant gardens of the Hudson Valley. Here you will find a vast array of flowers, sculptures and other natural beauty in rocks, trees and water features. If you plan on going here's a few tips. Avoid windy days. If you want to get those sharp images of plant life it is easiest if they are not blowing around. Bring a macro lens. You'll find that the macro world is teaming with interesting detail. You'll want to capture this up close. The eye of a grasshopper, the stigma of a flower, the veins of a leaf all are wondrous and make captivating photos. Bring a spray bottle of water to give the flowers a little spritz. Water drops add interest to plants. If you go early you may happen across a dew soaked spider web. Birds and Butterflies and other insects frequent gardens so be ready and observant. Bring your tripod and your telephoto lens too. You don't know what awaits you in the garden. Be ready.

2 1/2 acres of Poinsettias on Wessels' Farms in Otisville.
Canon 7D, 125mm, 1/200 @f5.6 ISO 800, EV -1, saturation -1, tone -1

Roadside Fields
Although manicured gardens like the Orange County Arboretum provide easy access to flowers and other plants, unkept fields can hold their own surprises. Wild flowers and the natural landscape have their own beauty without the obvious man-made feel. Be careful not to wonder onto private property while driving around looking for shots to hang on your wall.

Left: A small grasshopper suns himself atop a Denver Daisy at the Orange County Arboretum

Below: A Monarch Butterfly hangs from a tuft of Goldenrod in a roadside field

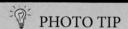

PHOTO TIP

Many species of butterflies begin to emerge from their chrysalis by Mother's Day when it is still chilly in the morning. This is a great time to visit the butterfly houses of the Hudson Valley. Butterflies are not very active below 60 degrees and are much easier to approach. If you place your finger directly in front of the butterfly and gently push back against the insect's legs it will walk right up onto your finger. You can now place the butterfly where you prefer to take the shot. It would be considerate to ask permission before handling any butterflies.

Previous Pages: A stand of green leafy plants pay homage to a boulder crowned with ivory at Innisfree Garden, Millbrook: Canon 7D, 31mm, 1/30sec @ f25, ISO100
Appalachian Trail Pochuck Boardwalk near Wawayanda State Park, NJ
Canon 7D, 32mm, 1/50sec @ f14, ISO 100

Hudson Valley Gardens:

Bard College	Red Hook	Dutchess County	
Donald M Kendall Sculpture Gardens	Purchase	Westchester County	
Innisfree Garden	Millbrook	Dutchess County	30
Locust Grove	Poughkeepsie	Dutchess County	
Opus 40	Saugerties	Ulster County	
Orange County Arboretum	Montgomery	Orange County	29, 33, 34
Roosevelt Mansion	Hyde Park	Dutchess County	
Stonecrop Gardens	Cold Spring	Putnam County	
Storm King Art Center	Cornwall	Orange County	
Vanderbilt Mansion	Hyde Park	Dutchess County	

Northern New Jersey sunflower farms
Canon 7D, 70mm, 1/20 @ f22, ISO 100

Facing page: Orange County Arboretum, Montgomery
Canon 7D, 50mm, 1/200sec @ f8, ISO 200

FOCUS POINTS

One of my biggest frustrations with the camera is automatic focus. I love auto focus but I hate it when the camera focuses in the wrong place. How can the camera know what I want to focus on? It can't. No matter how technically advanced cameras become they will never be able to read my mind. Look at the photos of the dice on the next page. There are three dice in each photograph and a different die is focused on in each. A student of mine was photographing a hawk that had just landed in his back yard. He grabbed his camera and snapped a shot letting the camera decide where to focus. It looked great on the back screen of the camera. Long after the hawk had flown away, he looked at the photograph on the larger computer screen and found that the camera had focused on a branch a few feet in front of the hawk and the hawk itself was not sharp. The shot was ruined. The camera does not know the difference between a hawk and a branch. It can't determine the best esthetic arrangement of objects in and out of focus. Your best option is to learn how to control your focus points.

Focus points are the little squares you see light up in your view finder or on your LCD display when you press the shutter release button half way down. When your auto focus (AF) setting is set to select your focus points automatically the camera's computer will look at the information at each one of these points. Digital cameras need contrast to focus. If there is no contrast under a focus point the camera will ignore it. The points that have contrast under them will be compared using a programmed algorithm. This algorithm is based on typical untrained photographer habits. An average camera wielder will place the subject in the center and closest to the camera which is why your camera focuses on objects that are closest to the camera and the center of the image. This is the reason the camera focused on the branch and not the hawk.

Last die in focus

Middle die in focus

First die in focus

As your photography skills improve and you begin to place your subjects away from the center of the image and choose subjects that are not closest to the camera you will find these basic algorithms to be inadequate. Look at the Globe Thistle photo on the facing page. The thistles on the right are up close to the camera but I chose to focus on the one further away. To accomplish this you must set your camera's settings to single focus point. Most cameras use the rear buttons or dial to change between each focus point. You must select a focus point that is touching the area of the photograph you wish to be in focus. If you use single focus points you must be aware of which focus point is selected at all times and move it for every picture. This can be tedious to a beginner but becomes second nature quickly. You will find that your photographs will improve tremendously.

Our cameras are improving and automatic modes are getting better at detecting our subjects. Face detect works extremely well in many compact cameras when you are taking snapshots of people but once you begin to take control, all that automatic stuff just gets in the way.

Dutchess County Balloon Festival - Walkway over the Hudson in background
Canon 7D, 100mm, 1/256 @ f8, ISO 400

Did you ever chase down a hot air balloon to get a nice picture? I have. And although it was a lot of fun, it makes more sense to visit someplace where many balloons are launched together. There are many hot air balloon festivals around the country and the closest one in the Hudson Valley is the Dutchess County Balloon Festival in Poughkeepsie. Each year in July a dozen or so balloons are launched near Waryas park. There are great views of the spectacle from the Walkway Over the Hudson. Boaters gather on the river to watch from their vessels. Set your alarm clock and grab your camera. It's going to be a great photo opportunity.

PHOTO TIP

Apply the "Rule of Thirds" to your photos. Basically what the rule of thirds says is "Do not place your subject in the center of your photograph". Image a tick-tack-toe grid over your viewfinder. Some cameras have a setting that overlays this grid onto your image. Now place your subject where the lines cross. If you have a long subject such as a bridge or horizon, place that along one of the horizontal or vertical lines in the grid. You photos will improve tremendously.

Facing page: Dutchess County Balloon Festival - Blowing up the balloons
Canon 7D, 18mm, 1/60 @ f5.6, ISO 400

The circle of confusion is simply a spot where light rays come together on the digital sensor of your camera. Most people probably won't consider learning about it a worth while use of time. But, learning about the circle of confusion will help you to understand some very useful and interesting aspects of digital photography. Things like depth-of-field, lens resolution, sharpness and bokeh all are related to the circle of confusion.

How sharp is your lens?

First, what is focus? I mean, what actually happens to the light as it bounces off an object and enters your camera focused or out-of-focus?

To understand focus you need to understand how light rays find and enter your camera's lens. It is important to understand that light travels in a straight line. You can only see light that is directed straight at you. If you shine a flashlight in the dark you cannot see the beam of light unless it is pointed right into your eyes. You can only see what the beam of light hits. Once a ray of light hits the surface of an object, it bounces off in an infinite number of directions, dispersing the light so everybody around can see it. This is due to the imperfections of the surface material the object is made of (see figure above).

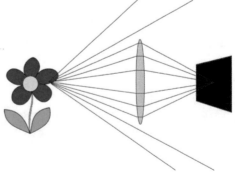

This is where your camera's lens goes to work. Its job is to collect as much of that light as possible and focus it onto the camera's light sensitive chip (CCD). Every ray of light that hits the subject bounces in a different direction. There are trillions of light-rays shooting off the object you are photographing. Only a small portion of that light actually makes it directly into your camera but even that small percentage of light rays is a very large number. This light enters through the lens as cone shaped points of light which take the size and shape of the aperture and focus down to a tiny point on the CCD. The smaller the point, the sharper the image (see figure to the right).

The point where these lines hit the CCD is known as the circle of confusion. The size of this area depends on how much the point is in focus. The sharper the focus, the finer the point. An out-of-focus point will be much larger.

Spherical aberrations

Yes, we mentioned this earlier but now is a good time to revisit the topic. The finer the focal point, the sharper the image. But how fine can this point be? That depends on the quality of the lens. The problem is that the rate light bends as it passes through a lens at different angles is not a constant. The greater the angle between the light ray and the lens surface at the entry point, the greater the change of angle as it passes through the glass. This means that the rays of light that pass through the lens at its outer edge bends more than the light that enters in through the center. Yes, we expect this to happen but look at the diagram to see what I mean. The light rays towards the outside edges are bending too much so that they are not all meeting at one fine point. This makes the sharp tip of the cone of light dull. It's like drawing with a dull pencil. No matter how hard you try, you can't draw sharp lines. This is know as spherical aberration. No matter how much you try, you cannot focus down to the smallest point at the tip of the cone.

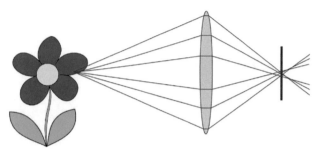

There are ways lens manufacturers can design lenses that will minimize spherical aberrations but this brings the cost of the lens up. If your lens is not creating sharp images, it could mean that it is suffering from severe spherical aberrations. Sharpness is not the only thing to be concerned about. There are also resolution concerns.

Lens Resolution

Let's assume we have a camera with a CCD resolution of 100 pixels. Yes, that is very low but it makes it easy for us to see what is going on. Now let's assume we have a basic stock lens with some spherical aberrations. Take a look at the diagram here. The smallest point we can focus 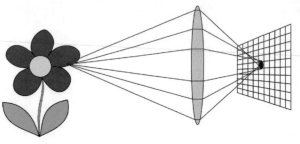 down to actually fills in one pixel on the CCD. This means that our lens is matched in resolution quality with our camera.

Lens Resolution vs camera resolution

Now we buy a new, higher resolution camera but we keep the same old lens. Our camera resolution is now 400 pixels. Look at the diagram. Our old lens cannot focus to a small enough point to cover one pixel. It takes four or more pixels to cover the smallest point of focus. Even though we improved our camera 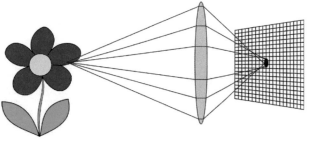 resolution, our photographs will not be any sharper because our lens cannot focus down to a fine enough point that will take advantage of the extra pixels our camera can capture.

So at times it may be wiser to upgrade your lens rather than upgrading your camera. What does this say about those new cell phone cameras that go up to 40 mega pixels? I have seen reviews that showed these cameras are no sharper than a 12 Mega pixel digital SLR camera. But that is still impressive for a cell phone.

The same thing applies to upgrading your lens when your camera cannot produce the resolution. A high quality lens capable of producing a very sharp image will be wasted on a camera with a low resolution sensor. The CCD will not be able to capture the sharpness the lens is capable of because our lens cannot focus down to a fine enough point that will take advantage of the extra pixels our camera can capture.

What is Bokeh?

Bokeh describes the rendition of out-of-focus points of light. Bokeh is different from sharpness. Sharpness is what happens at the point of best focus. Bokeh is what happens away from the point of best focus.

Every tiny area of your subject is sending light to your camera, from your main subject that you focused on to background and foreground subjects that are out of focus. Those points that are out of focus miss the CCD in your camera and actually focus in front of or behind the CCD. This means that the cone from those points of light did not come to it's smallest point on the CCD. These points of light get spread across the CCD in a larger area known as the circle of confusion. The further the point is from sharp focus, the larger the area of confusion. These out of focus cones of light overlap each other causing what we know as blur. The larger the area of confusion, the more blur (see figure above).

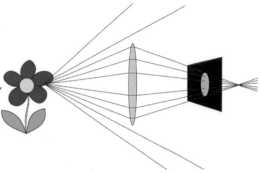

It is important to note here that this area of confusion takes the exact shape of your aperture. If your aperture is wide open they will be perfectly round. This is not usually noticeable because there are millions of these points overlapping each other in the blurred parts of your photo usually resulting in a pleasing blur. However, when there is very high contrast in your blurred area such as a small point of light, the area of confusion for that point will be very distinct.

A high quality lens has the ability to create sharp images by focusing on a very tiny tip of these cones of light while at the same time producing a soft blur around the larger, out-of-focus points. Some low quality lenses are unable to obtain such a sharp focus due to imperfect lenses which cause spherical aberrations. This prevents the lens from reaching the finest points on each cone of light. Your camera may be able to capture an extremely high resolution but without a lens capable of focusing down to a small enough point you still cannot obtain the sharpest image your CCD may be capable of.

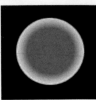

Poor Bokeh. This is a greatly magnified blur circle known as the circle of confusion. It shows very poor bokeh. A blur circle is how an out-of-focus point of light is rendered. Note how the edge is sharply defined and even emphasized for a point that is supposed to be out-of-focus, and that the center is dark.

Neutral Bokeh. This is a technically perfect and evenly illuminated blur circle. Although it has the blur we want it still does not produce a good bokeh, because the edge is still well defined. Out-of-focus objects, either points of light or lines, can effectively create reasonably sharp lines in the image due to the edges of the sharp blur circle. This is a blur circle from most modern lenses designed to be "perfect"

Good Bokeh. Here is what we want. This is great for bokeh since the edge is completely undefined. This also is the result of the same spherical aberration, but in the opposite direction, of the poor example seen in Fig. 1. This is where art and engineering start to diverge, since the better looking image is the result of an imperfection. Perfect bokeh demands a Gaussian blur circle distribution, and lenses are designed for the neutral example shown in the second image.

 PHOTO TIP

Bad Orbs

Just as out-of-focus points of lights can create eye catching backgrounds they can also ruin a photo in some ways. This usually happens when on camera flash is used. Often there are small particles of dust floating in the air. Rain drops and snow flakes can be culprits too but dust is the big one because you don't know it's there when you take the photograph. The camera's on board flash lights up the tiny specks of dust when the photo is snapped. But dust is so tiny, how can it ruin a photo? That dust particle is much closer to the camera than your subject is so that means it is out of focus. What happens to tiny points of light when they are out of focus? They become larger orbs. Some people believe they have caught a spirit in the photograph. Actually all that has happened is they caught a piece of dust in the air. This can be proven. Put your camera on a tripod and turn on your flash. Snap a photo of something about 20 or 30 feet away from the camera. Now take a pillow and punch it with your fist a few times right in front of the camera. Take another photo. You have just proven that those orbs are just dust out of focus lit up by your flash.

Background, just as important as foreground

When you look at an object not only does your eye automatically focus on the object you are viewing but your brain does as well. It is very difficult to gaze on a particular object but watch some other activity elsewhere through the "corner of your eye". This is not typical behavior. We naturally turn our heads and focus our eye on what our mind is focused on, ignoring everything else. This is quite different in photography. Once the shot has been captured, printed and is now being viewed, the spectator can focus on all parts of the image, including those that are not of the subject. Yes, one can observe the out-of-focus backgrounds and corners. So it is important to capture those properly. Just as import as the subject. You must train yourself to study every single aspect of the scene you are shooting, including backgrounds and edges.

The photo above on the left was taken with a low to mid quality lens. Notice the out-of-focus branches in the background of the photo. Even though the branches are out of focus, the edges are still distinct. The branch simply got thicker. This happens because the area of confusion in the out-of-focus points of light has a distinct edge. It is most noticeable when there are objects with high contrast between its edge and the background. It can have an undesirable effect on your photographs.

This sharp edge of bokeh is not usually noticeable when there are millions of points of similar contrast mixed together. It is only noticeable when there is a large contrast difference between points such as small lights or light reflecting from shiny surfaces. One way to prevent this from happening without upgrading to expensive lenses is to simply choose your backgrounds more carefully. Find an angle for the shot that has a more analogous background without the contrasty straight lines such as in the photo above on the right.

Out-of-Focus Points of Light
Those small high contrast, out of focus points of lights in your photograph can be used to your advantage in an artistic way. Because objects that are out of focus keep a sharp edge around them, small points of light become large orbs with a soft, creamy body.

These out of focus points of lights can be an unusual, pleasing backdrop to a photo. Strings of Christmas lights are commonly used to create large orbs of light in the background of your photos. With a little creative composition you can make the orbs in the background appear to be inter-acting with your foreground. The lights in these photos are about 20 feet behind the foreground subject.

The trick to creating these orbs is:
   1) Make sure there is a large distance between the foreground and background.
   2) Use the largest aperture your lens is capable of. The best way to achieve this is to use aperture priority mode.
   3) Focus on a subject as close to the lens as possible. Remember, every lens has a minimum focus distance. If you get too close to your subject the lens will not be able to focus. Only macro lenses can get up close to your subject. If your lens won't get a focus lock, back up a little and try again.

Christmas Orbs
Yes, this is the trick used to get those large colorful orbs from Christmas lights and sun reflecting in water drops.

The Shape of Bokeh

An interesting thing about bokeh. The out-of-focus lights take the shape of the lens' aperture. When the aperture is wide open it creates a perfectly round circle but when the aperture is closed down, several leaflets fold in among themselves creating a hexagonal shape. Each point of light will become this shape. Wouldn't it be great if we can make the aperture any shape we wanted?

There is a way you can make your own aperture. All you have to do is make a paper cover for your lens with the shape you want punched right in the center.

First, Cut a strip of black paper, wrap it around the lens and tape the ends to form a loop.

Second, cut a round circular disk from the black paper the exact diameter of the loop you made.

Next, punch a shape in the center of the disk. It is critical that the shape is absolutely in the center of the disk.

Tape the disk to one end of the loop and push it onto the lens.

That sounds easy but there are a few catches. How are you going to punch a hole in the center of the disk when most hole punches only punch close to the edge of the paper? You'll have to cut a crude hole with scissors then punch the edge of a smaller piece of paper that you will tape over the hole.

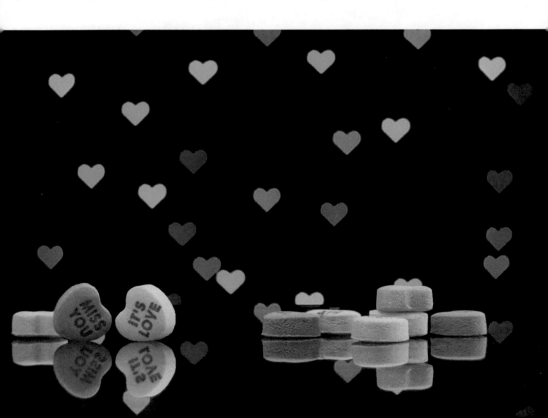

Where are you going to get those hole punches? That's an easy one. Those chain craft stores have tons of them.

How large should the hole be? That depends on your lens. For most lenses 10mm will work well but there is a formula if you want to get technical: lens focal length divided by the lens' maximum aperture. Example: a 50mm f1.8 will be 50 / 1.8 = 27.7mm or smaller. Lenses with a larger aperture work best.

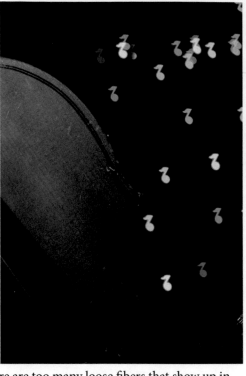

Some important details:
1) Keep the aperture as wide open as it can go.
2) Prime lenses work best but if you use a zoom, make sure you are zoomed in all the way.
3) Place your foreground object as close to the lens as possible and still be able to focus on it. This will give you the largest shapes.
4) When making your aperture lens cover do not use ordinary construction paper. There are too many loose fibers that show up in the photo. Use scrapbooking card stock.
5) Make sure the hole you punch is exactly in the center.
6) Don't make the hole too large. If it is too large, it will not work.
7) Dim the room lights and use a tripod

BRIDGES

Perrine's Bridge, the second oldest covered bridge in the State of New York. The bridge spans the Wallkill River right along side the New York State Thruway (I87). It's location is about 5 miles north of New Paltz just off Route 32 along Route 213. It was built in 1835 and is 138 feet long. The bridge is named from James W Perrine who owned an inn on the east side of the bridge. Perrine's son was hired each year as the "snower". It was his job to spread snow across the bridge so that horse drawn sleighs could cross. Maps show the area across the street as Perrine's Park but it is just a wooded area. As you travel Route 213 from Route 32 to the bridge you'll see a small park on the Wallkill River with picnic tables. This is a great place to have your lunch while visiting Perrine's Bridge.

Perrine's Covered Bridge
Canon 7D, 18mm, 1/250 @ f8.0, ISO 800, HDR

Franny Reese State Park

I've been driving across the Mid-Hudson bridge for years and never realized that just a few hundred feet above the road in the treeline was an overlook where people took in the view of the bridge as traffic sped to and fro. This overlook is the main attraction of Franny Reese State Park. Other curiosities in the park include the ruins of an old estate.

Cedar Glen was a Victorian mansion built in 1868 by Dr. Charles H. Roberts. Roberts held a doctorates in dentistry and invented an anesthetic and false teeth made from porcelain which earned him enough money to invest in the railroad during the mid 1800's. In the early 1900's around the time of his death, there was turmoil between his children as they fought for control over his estate. Apparently things didn't go well and the estate was abandoned when the main access road was cut off with the construction of the mid-Hudson bridge. Slowly the estate fell to ruins and forgotten about as nature reclaimed the land. Remains of the mansion and other buildings can be seen from the trails that run through the park. Much of the land and buildings were destroyed as the land was developed into new homes but further development was stopped and the remaining land purchased by the Scenic Hudson Park Service. The park is named after Frances "Franny" Reese who was renowned for leading the battle against Consolidated Edison's (ConEd) 1963 plan to build a hydroelectric pump storage facility into the side of Storm King Mountain. Her efforts were triumphant and the facility that would have destroyed much of the hiking area we enjoy today was never built.

Bear Mountain Bridge from the foot bridge.   *Facing page: Franny Reese State Park, Highland*
Canon 7D, 30mm, 30 seconds @f22 ISO 400, EV +0.7   Canon 7D, 124s @ f11

EXPOSURE COMPENSATION

A properly exposed photo recreates the image with the same brightness as you see with your eye. For example, if I photograph a black sheet of paper the image created should be just that, a black sheet of paper, not a gray piece of paper. The problem is that the camera has no way to know what you are photographing, a black sheet of paper or a white sheet of paper. If you had in an empty room with one main light on the ceiling that illuminates the entire room evenly, and painted one wall solid black and the opposite wall solid white, then photographed both walls allowing the camera to calculate the exposure, and printed those photos out to look at side by side, you would not be able to tell which was which. They would both be gray. In fact, the camera assumes that everything you photograph is gray. To be more exact, middle gray or 18% gray. I'll prove it. I placed a white sheet of paper and a black sheet of paper on the table. I set my camera to program mode which means the camera will automatically calculate the exposure, put the focus on manual because the camera is unable to focus without contrast and zoomed to fill the frame entirely with the black sheet of paper. I snapped the shutter. Then I switched and photographed the white sheet. I posted both pictures below. Which one is the white paper and which one is the black?

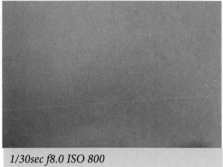

1/30sec f8.0 ISO 800

1/2sec f8.0 ISO 800

If your camera has a dynamic meter mode such as matrix or evaluative it may do a little better than what you see above but no where near what black and white should be.

So what went wrong? Nothing. The camera worked just as it is supposed to. The camera's light meter measures reflected light. The white sheet of paper reflected more light back at the camera so the computer in the camera increased the shutter speed causing the image to underexpose and produce a gray sheet of paper. In the second photo the black sheet of paper reflected very little light back to the camera so the camera's computer decreased the shutter speed causing the image to over expose and produce a gray sheet of paper.

The best way to determine the correct exposure is to measure incident light, the light that is hitting the subject, not the light that is reflecting off the subject. Since the light didn't change between photographing each sheet of paper, the exposure settings should not have changed as we saw in the above example. To obtain the correct image, the exposure values should remain the same as depicted on the next page.

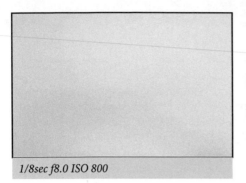
1/8sec f8.0 ISO 800

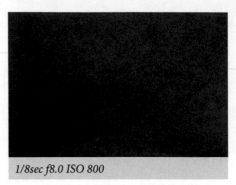
1/8sec f8.0 ISO 800

Unfortunately the only way to measure incident light is to purchase an incident light meter, then enter the settings into the camera manually. But the camera provides us with other ways to obtain a good exposure. One of which is called exposure compensation.

So, how does exposure compensation work? Remember back when we learned about exposure stops? Now you will be using those. On the previous page the white sheet of paper image had a shutter speed of 1/30 of a second. The correct exposure was determined to be 1/8 of a second as depicted above. Let's do a little math: Double 1/30 and you get 1/15. That's one stop. Double 1/15 and you get 1/7.5 which is actually `1/8. That makes two stops. The correct exposure is two stops above the exposure the camera calculated. We must compensate the exposure by +2 stops.

To set exposure compensation, first you must be in a camera mode that allows you to adjust this setting. Those modes are *Program* (P), *Shutter Priority* (S or Tv), and *Aperture Priority* (A or Av). Next, find the exposure compensation (Av) button on the camera or setting in the menu. It is often a button like the one pictured here. This button will activate a slider like the one shown below or on some cameras you'll just see the number it is set to.
By simultaneously holding down the Av button and turning the command dial the indicator will adjust up and down the scale in 1/3 stop increments.

What is actually happening here is your are adding or subtracting exposure from whatever exposure settings the camera is automatically calculating. You are compensating the camera's automatic exposure. The camera is still working automatically for you. You don't have to purchase extra equipment or make manual exposure guesses. You simply subtract exposure compensation when you are photographing something that is very dark or add exposure compensation when you are photographing something that is very bright.

Let's do a couple examples...

With the camera set to program mode and exposure compensation set to neutral (0) I setup some black dice on a black sheet of paper and snapped the photo. It is grossly over exposed. Since the photograph is darker than middle gray and the camera assumes that every photo is middle gray it over exposed the dark image to make it gray. Since the photo is over exposed I need to compensate for the error and set exposure compensation to under expose the image.

I chose to under expose the image by -1.3 stops and got these final results. The image now looks a lot more like the actual subject. OK, so who wants to photograph black dice on black paper or white dice on white paper. I have to admit, that doesn't come along all that often but similar things happen more often than you know. What about snow? Or a white wedding gown? Or your black lab? You may not be adjusting the exposure by 2

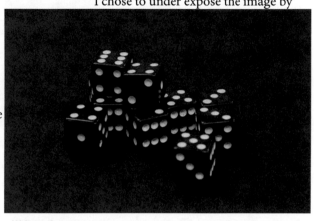

stops that often but very often you'll be adjusting it 1/3 or 2/3 stops or maybe even 1 and you'll see a difference. Nobody wants their whites to come out of the washer gray. Why would you want the white in your photographs to be gray?

The camera sees your photograph as if it is a wet oil painting with all the colors smeared together but viewed in black and white. Imagine your photo like this. What shade of gray is it? When you photograph something that is darker than middle gray, set exposure compensation in the negative direction. If you photograph something that is lighter than middle gray, set exposure compensation in the positive direction.

Exposure Compensation: 0.0

Exposure Compensation: +1.7

The Bright Sunny Day Conspiracy

Exposure Compensation issues don't only affect light and dark colored objects. They also wreak havoc on lighting conditions. The camera assumes everything is a bright sunny day. Shoot in a dimly lit restaurant and the camera makes it like a bright sunny day. Shoot during an evening stroll by the lake and the camera makes it like a bright sunny day. Shoot a sunset and the camera makes it like a bright sunny day. Everything you shoot is a bright sunny day. Sometimes we don't mind that the camera brightens up the shot but when you want to capture the dimly lit scene it can be a big problem. Exposure Compensation comes to the rescue. To keep the darkened ambiance of the scene, dial down the exposure compensation.

Less is More

Light is additive. When working with photography you are working with light. As more light is added it becomes brighter, lighter, whiter. Therefore if your photo is not exposed properly, that is over exposed, the photo will become *washed out*, devoid of color.

If your photos look dismal and bleak, lacking vibrance in color it could be that the photo is over exposed. Dial down the exposure compensation a tad bit to help brighten up the colors. This happens frequently when photographing fall foliage. When you stand there looking at the scene you see lots of color but for some reason the camera just doesn't grab it. You've heard people say "the photo doesn't do it justice". Why is that? First of all, if you are out and about looking at fall colors it's probably a nice sunny day. The pictures are simply too bright. Use the exposure compensation feature and under expose the photo a tad bit. It'll help.

The blue Robin's eggs in the nest above are washed out because the light was too harsh. Bringing the exposure compensation down a little will help this. We also blocked the direct sunlight with a sheet.

HISTORIC BUILDINGS

Gomez Mill House in Milton
Canon 7D, 18mm, 1/2 @ f22, ISO 400, EV -1, saturation +3

Historic buildings abound in this part of the country. Check the internet or some of the popular local magazines to find numerous places to photograph old buildings. Every town has them. Another good source is your local historian. Each county has a historian and they are usually very quick to discuss historic places with you. You may even learn of a unique place with limited access. Sometimes the hunt is as rewarding as getting the photograph.

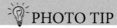
PHOTO TIP

Photographing buildings is challenging due to perspective distortion. If you are lucky enough to own a tilt shift lens this will solve the distortion problem. Unfortunately we all don't have such a generous budget. You can perform a little postproduction with programs such as Photoshop to help correct the distortion. Another way to rid the distortion is to get back and take the photograph from a distance.

First Presbyterian Church at Church Park, Goshen
Canon 7D, 18mm, 6sec @ f11, ISO 800

Hudson Valley Historic Buildings:

Location	Town	County	Page
Brotherhood Winery	Washingtonville	Orange County	
Church Park www.fpgoshen.org	Goshen	Orange County	57
Cragsmoor Stone Church www.cragsmoorstonechurch.org	Cragsmoor	Ulster County	58, 59
Croton Dam parks.westchestergov.com/croton-gorge-park	Croton	Westchester County	
Dennings Point	Beacon	Dutchess County	
Fort Montgomery www.nysparks.com/historic-sites/28/details.aspx	Fort Montgomery	Orange County	49, 109
Gomez Mill House www.gomez.org	Milton	Orange County	56
Locust Grove	Poughkeepsie	Dutchess County	
Museum Village	Monroe	Orange County	
Roosevelt Mansion	Hyde Park	Dutchess County	
Slaatsburgh State Historic Site	Poughkeepsie	Dutchess County	
Snyder Estate Natural Cement Historic District	Rosendale	Ulster County	
Vanderbilt Mansion	Hyde Park	Dutchess County	
West Point Foundry Preserve	Cold Spring	Putnam County	

Stone church in Cragsmoor
Canon 7D, 18mm, 20 seconds @ f8 ISO 100

Eye Camera

Dynamic Range is the amount of light between the darkest value and the lightest value that the camera can capture. The human eye can see about 24 stops of dynamic range, twice what a good quality camera can capture as seen in the chart to the right. Cheaper cameras only capture about 5 stops of dynamic range. Detail that you can see with your eye in the dark and light areas may become solid black or solid white in the photo that the camera captures. This means that some of the detail that you see in the scene you are photographing may not be exposed properly. This happens in scenes where there is both dark and light areas. Look at the image of the bridge above. The bridge is dark and the clouds are light. The camera is not able to capture all the detail in both the dark and light areas. In this example the camera lightened the entire image to expose the darker bridge properly but the clouds are blown out. This is not only obvious in the photograph but in the histogram as well. The darker bridge exposure can be seen on the left side of the histogram. All the detail is captured well. The clouds show up on the right side. Notice that they are crushed to the right edge, much of it being pure white. This shows that detail in the sky was lost.

Below the image was underexposed by 2 stops. Examining the image and histogram we see that the detail in the clouds are now prevalent.

The darker foreground of the image shows in the histogram on the left side. The lighter clouds are spread from middle to right. We now see great detail in the clouds but lose it in the structure. One picture cannot capture the entire dynamic range however, two or three can. We just have to figure out a way to combine them together and make one good exposure as seen below. This is called High Dynamic Range or HDR photography.

Bracketing

Capturing three separate images at three different exposures automatically is called *Automatic Exposure Bracketing* (AEB). Most digital SLR cameras have this option, however setting it up differs between camera makes and models.

You can get to it through Canon's *Q* menu and through Nikons *i* menu and selecting the AEB or Exposure compensation option. The default number of images the camera will take is three but on some cameras this can be changed to five in the camera's advanced custom settings menu.

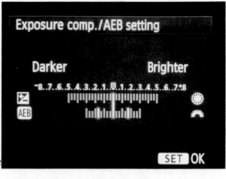

Three is usually adequate. Using the camer'as command dial you can adjust how far apart you want each exposure. To take the pictures simply press the camera's shutter release button, the camera will do the rest. When the shutter release mode is set to one-shot you will need to take three separate photos one at a time. The camera will automatically adjust the exposure compensation for each image. An indicator in the viewfinder and the back display will show which exposure is being taken. To simplify things you can set the shutter release mode to continuous and hold down the shutter to take all three shots one right after the other. The camera will stop shooting after the third picture even though the shut-

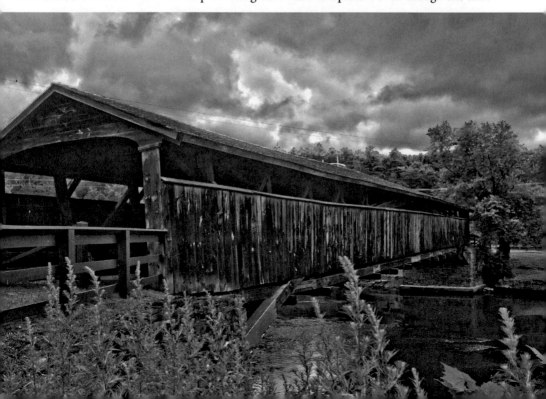

ter release is set to continuous shooting. Some software can automatically align the three shots but it is best to use a tripod so each image is identical. When using a tripod it is best to set the self timer so you can move your hands away from the camera before the photos are taken. This prevents any camera shake caused by touching the camera. Some cameras will even take all three bracketed shots automatically when in the self timer mode. If your camera doesn't have any settings for Auto Exposure Bracketing you'll simply have to set the exposure compensation manually for each image and take the shots one at a time. As you can see, taking three bracketed shots for HDR can be very different between camera makes and models. You'll have to experiment to find the best way to use your own camera.

HDR Software
Once you've taken three shots at three different exposures you'll have to use software such as Adobe Photoshop or Photomatrix Pro to combine them as an HDR image. Some cameras have an HDR option built in but it will be limited compared to software on the computer. There are a myriad of other options in the software such as sharpness, strength, saturation, gamma and much more. The image of the truck below and Bannerman's Castle on the next page are HDR photographs along with many others in this book.

Old Truck in field, Ulster County
Canon 7D, 18mm, 1/40sec @ f10, ISO 200, HDR

Facing Page: Bannerman's Island Arsenal
Canon T3i, 55mm, 1/250sec @ f10, ISO 400, HDR

Photo by Kevin Kreischer - Canon 5D 560mm 1/20s @ f8

Visit the great wetland parks of the Hudson Valley including the Bashakill along route 209 in Sullivan County or Stewart State Forest in Orange County or Constitution Marsh in Cold Spring. Bring along your telephoto lens. Wildlife in the Hudson Valley is shy and doesn't give you much of a chance to get up close.

Bald Eagle numbers are increasing in the Hudson Valley. By the 1930's people became aware of the diminishing bald eagle population and began taking steps to protect them. The Bald Eagle Act was passed in 1940 which helped make it possible for their population to recover. DDT and other pesticides were a major cause in destroying these magnificent birds. Large quantities of DDT were discovered in dead eagles. Bald Eagles were officially declared an endangered species in 1967. A handful of species made it back off the endangered species list and can be seen frequently in the Hudson River Valley.

West end of the Bashakill
Canon 7D, 18mm, 1/128 @ f6.4, ISO 200, color saturation +2, EV +1

Constitution Marsh, Cold Spring
Canon 7D, 18mm, 1/200sec @ f9, ISO 100

Taken from the Appalachian Trail, Vernon, NJ
Canon 7D, 105mm, 1/26sec @ f14, ISO 100

Wetlands of the Hudson Valley:

Location	Town	County
Bashakill Marsh	Wurtsboro	Sullivan County, pg 64
Constitution Marsh	Cold Spring	Putnam County, pg 65
Goose Pond Mountain	Monroe	Orange County
Great Swamp	Pawling	Dutchess County
Hunter Farm Preserve	Slate Hill	Orange County
Manitou Point Preserve	Garrison	Putnam County
Nuclear Lake	Pawling	Dutchess County
Stewart State Forest	Maybrook	Orange County, pg 66

Horse Friendly Parks:

Goose Pond Mountain	Monroe	Orange County
Highland Lakes State Park	Scotchtown	Orange County
Minnewaska Preserve	Shawangunk	Ulster County
Mohonk Preserve	Shawangunk	Ulster County
Stewart State Forest	Maybrook	Orange County, pg 66
Trotters Track	Goshen	Orange County, pg 13, 69

North American Box Turtle at Stewart State Forest, Maybrook
Canon 20D, 55mm, 1/40sec @ f5.6, ISO 100

Bulb Setting

Perhaps you want to take a long exposure beyond the maximum 30 second limit of your camera. Or perhaps you don't know how long the exposure will need to be and you want to adjust it on the fly. That is what the bulb setting is used for. As long as you hold down the shutter release, the shutter will stay open.

Some cameras have a bulb setting on the mode dial. On other cameras this setting can be found by placing the camera in full manual mode and adjusting the shutter speed as slow as it can go. The next click after 30 seconds is bulb. When using this long exposure feature it is best to have a remote control attached to your camera. A remote control, wired or wireless will prevent camera shake while you hold the shutter release down. Camera shake will blur your photograph especially during long exposures. Of course, a tripod is also required.

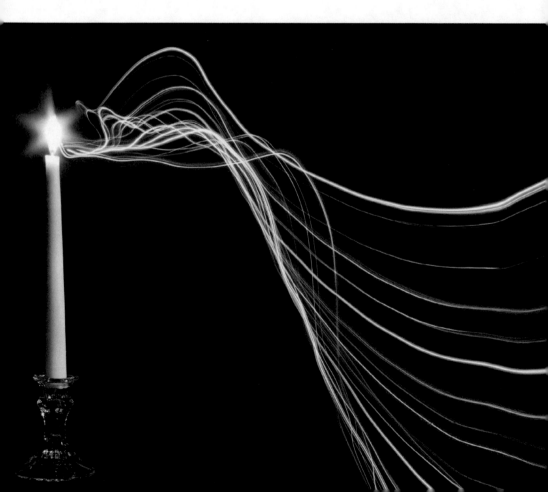

The Hudson Valley is renowned for their horse stables. You can't go too far without seeing horses in a pasture on a hillside somewhere. Visit the historic track and trotter's museum in Goshen. You can find trainers on the track with their horses year round.

If you are interested in photographing horses you might want to call ahead and arrange a visit. For an extensive list of stables in the Hudson Valley area visit www.itsaboutthehudsonvalley.com/stables/stables.html

 ## PHOTO TIP

Panning is a technique used by photographers to keep a moving object stationary relative to the camera. To pan with your camera simply follow the subject keeping it as stationary in the frame as possible. Start following the subject well before the proposed shot. Keep following as you squeeze the shutter release to take the photo and continue following a few seconds after the shot. From the camera's perspective the subject is not moving, the background is. If you use a relatively slow shutter speed such as 1/30th of a second, the background will blur as it zooms past. A blurred background will create the illusion of motion in your photograph.

Goshen Historic Track
Canon 7D, 70mm, 1/640sec @ f5.6, ISO 100

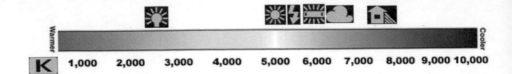

The wrong white balance can destroy a good picture. It is very important to understand the white balance setting in your camera. All cameras have a convenient Auto White Balance (AWB) setting but like many of the camera's automatic options, it is a guess. It is impossible for the camera to know what you are photographing. And sometimes the camera gets it wrong. One of the most problematic automatic settings on a digital camera is the auto white balance setting. It is always best to use the presets available under the white balance (WB) menu. Choose the preset that best matches the lighting condition you are shooting under and your whites will become more white.

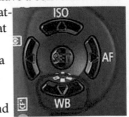

Both of these photos were taken under an incandescent (Tungsten) household light bulb.

White Balance set to automatic (AWB)

White Balance set to Tungsten

White Balance

AWB	Auto White Balance
	Tungsten
	Cloudy
	Sunny
	Flash
	Fluorescent
K	Kelvin
	Shade
	Custom

Refer to the chart near the top of the preceding page. This is a color graph of the kelvin temperature scale. Color temperature is based on the kelvin scale. You might say the color cast or hue in your photograph is based on degrees kelvin. The most pure white light comes from the sun. You can see this in the scale. Look at the sun symbol on the scale. The color under it is pure white. That means that when you set your camera's white balance to 'sun', all the white objects in your photograph will be white if you take the photograph under the sun.

Now, leaving your camera's white balance set to 'sun', take a photograph under a household incandescent light. Notice that every white object in your photograph will be yellow. This can be seen on the scale. Pure white is under the sun symbol. Look under the tungsten symbol. It is yellow.

Leaving your camera's white balance set to 'sun', find a shady spot outdoors and take a photograph. White objects will now be blue.

This color discrepancy is adjusted by selecting the correct white balance from your white balance presets.

If you leave your camera's white balance set to auto (AWB) the camera will try to do this for you automatically. Some camera makes and models perform better than others but few are accurate. All cameras perform better when the lighting condition is near the center of the scale. For quick snapshots automatic mode is adequate but for better photographs, choose the correct white balance.

Now examine the scale below. Here we set the camera's white balance to tungsten. Now all white objects under tungsten (incandescent household bulbs) will become white. But what will happen if we leave the white balance set to tungsten and go outside under the bright sun and take some photographs? You can see from the graph below that all those photos will become blue.

Warmer ———————————————————— Cooler

Taken from the top of Mount Beacon overlooking the Newburgh Beacon Bridge
Canon T3i, 27mm, 1/200 @ f8, ISO 100 - HDR

There are numerous hiking trails in the Hudson Valley. Books have been written on the subject. I can fill this book with photos of hiking trails. Some difficult, some easy, some with great vistas from high altitudes, some with exquisite forests and fields. Some you have to hike miles to reach the top while others you can drive to the top and sit in your car.

The best photographs are the ones that take work, like hiking to a view from the top of Schunemunk Mountain, the highest mountain in Orange County.

Trail maps to all the great views in the Hudson Valley can be obtained from the New York - New Jersey Trail Conference.

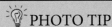 PHOTO TIP

Automatic camera modes are all based on typical behavior. Behaviors like placing your subject in the middle of your shot and keeping your subject as the closest object in your photo relative to the camera. Auto mode also assumes that your photo is taken during a bright sunny day. After all, who would take pictures in the rain or at night? You'll find that as your photography skills improve these automatic rules don't apply any longer. In fact, they begin to cause problems. One of these rules is the bright sunny day rule. When taking evening photos it is best to under expose your image using the Exposure Compensation (EV) adjustment. This will keep the color from washing out. Especially during sunsets.

Mount Beacon was literally a beacon during the Revolutionary War. Signal fires were lit on strategic mountain tops along the Hudson River to warn George Washington of British troop movements. A stone monument commemorating the signal fire stands on the mountain today. At the top of the mountain you'll find ruins of the Beacon Incline Railway, at one time the steepest funicular in the world. Stone foundations and a large concrete

Shawangunk Ridge

slab once part of a grand resort that was destroyed by a fire in 1983 provide an overlook of the Hudson River and the Catskill Mountains beyond. Nearby is also a fire tower where you can see all the way to Albany and New York City on a clear day. The trail to the top is steep but worth the climb.

Millbrook Mountain is the largest of the white cliffs viewed from roadways between Pine Bush and New Paltz. The best way to access the top of the cliff is through state owned Minnewaska Preserve along route 44/55. An old carriage road appropriately named Millbrook Carriage Road provides access via foot to the mountain. The view from the top is well

Millbrook Mountain

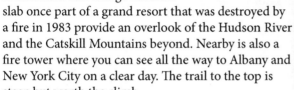

worth the walk and not as steep as one might think.

Schunemunk Mountain is the tallest mountain in Orange County at 1,664 feet above sea level. It is located in the town of Blooming Grove not far from Salisbury Mills. It offers a number of hiking trails with views of the valley. The Moodna Viaduct Railroad trestle runs across the valley at the base of the mountain. The trestle spans the valley for more than 3,200 feet and boasts being the longest railroad trestle east of the Mississippi River.

Schunemunk Mountain

Ruins of the old incline railroad on top of Mount Beacon
Canon T3i, f6.4, 28mm, ISO 100

A Port Jervis night scene taken from Elks Brox Memorial Park
Canon 7D, f18, 85mm, ISO 100

Storm King Mountain underwent a few name changes including Klinkesberg Mountain, named by Henry Hudson, and Boterberg or Butter Hill, named by early Dutch colonists. Storm King, proposed by writer Nathaniel Parker Willis finally stuck. Willis wrote "Standing aloft before other mountains in the chain, this sign is peculiar to him. He seems the monarch, and this seems his stately ordering of a change in the weather. Should not STORM-KING, then, be his proper title?"

Storm King Mountain

In 1965 the utility company Consolidated Edison (ConEd) wanted to create a pump storage power system on Storm King Mountain and nearby Black Rock Forest. The system would pump water from the Hudson River to a large reservoir during off peak hours when electric use was low then empty the reservoir through hydro generators during peek electric use. The idea was met with resistance from local activists who wanted to protect the aesthetic beauty of the area. ConEd eventually abandoned the idea.

The United States Military Academy used Storm King Mountain for artillery training during the late 19th century. Long after this practice was discontinued the mountain was opened to the public for recreational use. In 1999 unexploded ordinances were discovered after a forest fire cleared much of the forest debris. The mountain was closed to hiking for three years until it could be cleared of the danger.

Trails to an overlook of the Hudson River and Bannerman's Island can be accessed via a pull off on route 9W. Maps can be obtained from the New York - New Jersey Trail Conference.

Breakneck Ridge
Directly across the river stands Breakneck Ridge. The two mountains standing on opposite sides of the river form a wind gate. This area is known as the northern gateway to the Hudson Highlands. Breakneck is a 1,380 foot climb starting from a tunnel where route 9 penetrates the mountain. It is a strenuous hike with some rock scrambling and offers spectacular views of the Hudson River valley. The hike starts from a nearby parking area.

Breakneck Ridge

Shawangunk Ridge

Known simply as the "Gunks", the Shawangunk Ridge spans across Ulster County, Sullivan County and Orange County. It is a haven for rock climbers, bicyclists, hikers, skiers and visitors of all kinds from around the world. Some of the popular visitor spots include Sam's Point Preserve, Minnewaska State Preserve and Mohonk Preserve.
It is traversed by the Long path as well as many other hiking trails and old carriage roads. Many of the hiking trails are updated and maintained by the New York - New Jersey Trail Conference.

The Gunks are home to many waterfalls including 60 foot tall Awosting Falls in the Minnewaska Preserve. Awosting Falls can be accessed via an easy trail a short distance from the lower parking area.

Mohonk Preserve lookout tower

Eliminating Haze

The biggest problem with photographing mountain top landscapes is the blue/gray haze you get when photographing across a long distance. There may be no way to completely eliminate it without expensive post production software and plug-ins that remove haze but here are a few tricks. First, try using a UV and/or polarizer filter. These filters will help in reducing exposure from random stray light which tents to wash out your photograph. Try increasing the contrast and color saturation under your camera's Picture Control or Picture Styles menu. Use the proper white balance. Be careful here, if you warm the picture by using a cooler white balance such as shade you will just get yellow haze instead of blue or gray. For the advanced user you may try reducing the blue channel a little. The best time to photograph mountain scenes is when the humidity is low. If you're like me and you just hiked up a steep thousand foot slope you may no longer care if the photo has any haze.

Joppenbergh Mountain, Rosendale

Hiking in the Hudson Valley

There is walking and then there is hiking. Hiking is typically up steep inclines and along rocky paths. There are hundreds of miles of hiking trails in the Hudson Valley, Probably more like thousands, too many to list. Here is a list of some of the well known places:

Location	Town	County
Black Creek Preserve	Esopus	Ulster County
Black Rock Forest	Cornwall	Orange County
Breakneck Ridge	Cold Spring	Putnam County, pg 76
Clarence Fahnestock State Park	Hopewell Junction	Putnam County
Dater Mountain Natural park	Sloatsburg	Rockland County
Dunderberg Spiral Railway	Stony Point	Rockland County
Fishkill Ridge	Beacon	Dutchess County
Huckleberry Ridge State park	Port Jervis	Orange County
Manitou Point Preserve	Garrison	Putnam County
Minnewaska Preserve	Shawangunk	Ulster County
Mohonk Preserve	Shawangunk	Ulster County
Mount Beacon Park	Beacon	Dutchess County, pg 73
Nuclear Lake	Pawling	Dutchess County
Sam's Point Preserve	Cragsmoor	Ulster County
Schunnemunk Mountain	Salisbury Mills	Orange County
Storm King Mountain	Cornwall	Orange County

Walking Trails

If you would like a quieter, more relaxed walk, here is a list of some of the parks that boast having leisurely walking trails to name a few:

Burger Hill	Rhinebeck	Dutchess County
Constitution Marsh	Cold Spring	Putnam County
Dennings Point	Beacon	Dutchess County
Esopus Meadows Preserve	Port Ewen	Ulster County
Fort Montgomery	Fort Montgomery	Orange County, pg 49
Franny Reese State Park	Highland	Ulster County, pg 48
Fuller Mountain Preserve	Warwick	Orange County
Goose Pond Mountain	Monroe	Orange County
Great Swamp	Pawling	Dutchess County
Hunter Farm Preserve	Slate Hill	Orange County
Minnewaska Preserve	Shawangunk	Ulster County
Peach Hill Park	Poughkeepsie	Dutchess County
Poet's Walk	Red Hook	Dutchess County
Roosevelt Farm Lane Trail	Hyde Park	Dutchess County
Stone Church	Dover Plains	Dutchess County, pg 100
Storm King Art Center	Cornwall	Orange County
Stewart State Forest	Maybrook	Orange County

Color, color everywhere

Some pictures, though they may have captured the image as it actually is, scream "more color". The best way to enhance the color and contrast of your photographs is to use a professional image editing program however, for those who do not have such luxuries the camera provides ways to accomplish similar results. Digital SLR cameras often have Picture Style (Canon) or Picture Control (Nikon) options in the menu system. These settings allow you to adjust color saturation, hue, contrast and sharpness of your images.

After selecting *Picture Styles* from the shooting menu you will see a screen with several preset options: Canon uses Standard, Portrait, Landscape, Neutral, Faithful and Monochrome. Nikon uses Standard, Neutral, Vivid, Monochrome, Portrait and Landscape. Do not get these confused with the scene settings on the camera's mode dial. They have nothing to do with each other. The reason why there are several options to choose from is because you may decide to use different settings for different types of photos. For example, you may want your portraits to be a little soft and the hue adjusted for better skin tone. Or you may want landscapes to be a little sharper and adjust hue to bring out blues and greens. These settings are somewhat pre-programmed into the camera but can be further adjusted by changing Sharpness, Contrast, Saturation and Color tone after selecting the style. Nikon cameras have similar options under their *Picture Control* settings. Along with these preset styles both cameras also have user defined options.

Don't worry about moving the settings from their factory positions and forgetting where they belong. There is a *Default* button to return them to their original positions. Just press the button and the camera is back to the way it was before you played. I typically leave my camera set to the *Standard* style and increase both *Saturation* and *Sharpness*. Everybody has their own preference. Remember, these adjustments are permanent to jpg images but can be changed after the fact when shooting in RAW.

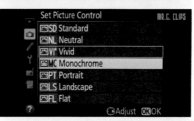

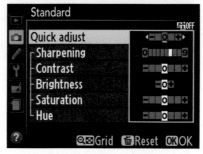

☀ PHOTO TIP

You can download more Picture Styles from Canon's Website and upload them to your camera including Nostalgia, Clear, Twilight, Autumn Hues and more.
web.canon.jp/imaging/picturestyle/file/

Although Picture styles can be used to tweak your photos in the camera, sometimes it is necessary to go a little further than the limits of the camera's built in adjustments. Some cameras have scene settings or effects settings that can add color along with other creative enhancements to your photos but these settings often place the camera into a full automatic mode which can be undesirable. To go the distance you will have to invest in photo editing software such as Photoshop or Lightroom. These programs can do amazing things to your photographs. Although some people believe that once a photo is tampered with it is no longer true art but there is more than one way to paint a rose. Who can say which is right and which is wrong? Below is a forgotten teddy bear that was leaning up against a concrete bridge support under the Thruway in New Paltz. The lighting under the bridge was very flat and the color in the bear was bleached out from sitting in water and in the sun. The graffiti also was old and faded. This was one of those pictures that needed help in the color saturation and contrast areas. I also added a bit of shadow for dramatic effect. As you can see in the images below, a little extra color can go a long way.

You do have to be careful not to go too far. Too much color saturation can do some pretty strange things.

On the next page there are three photos that benefitted from increased color saturation and contrast at various levels. These photos were very flat before the adjustment. Now they are alive with vivid color.

FAIRS, FESTIVALS AND CARNIVALS

Warwick Fireman's Festival
Canon 7D, 50mm, 1/160 @ f8, ISO 400, EV. -0.7, saturation +1

There is one thing that all carnivals have in common: color. And lots of it. Bring your tripod and remote control cable and join the fun. There are many fairs and carnivals throughout the Hudson Valley. Some of the more popular fairs are the county fairs such as the Orange County Fair, Ulster County Fair, Dutchess County Fair, Grahamsville Fair and the Warwick Fireman's Carnival. Carnivals are popular and can be found in almost every small town. Crowds are common so use caution if you decide to use a tripod.

Faster shutter speeds freeze motion while slower shutter speeds show motion blur. Look for the unusual. There is a lot to see at a carnival.

PHOTO TIP

Electric lights do not produce as much brightness as the sun. This means your shutter speed may be to too slow to hand hold your camera. In automatic mode your camera will compensate by raising your ISO thus increasing your shutter speed. You can adjust your ISO manually with the ISO button or camera menu. Be aware that a high ISO setting may cause unwanted distortion called noise in your photographs. It is best to use a tripod and keep your ISO down. If you need to freeze motion in a low light situation raising the ISO may be the only solution. Panning your subject may help as well.

Warwick Firemen's Carnival
Canon 7D, 125mm, 1/20s @ f5.6, ISO 800,
saturation +3

Warwick Firemen's Carnival
Canon 7D, 35mm, 1/2s @ f8, ISO 400, EV. +1,
saturation +3

Orange County Fair in Middletown, New York
Canon 7D, 35mm, 1/3 @ f5.6, ISO 100, EV. +1, saturation +2, contrast +2

Equipment

Other than your camera there are a few pieces of equipment that are a must when photographing fireworks.

     1) Tripod
     2) Remote shutter release

Frame the shot

Probably the most difficult part of photographing fireworks is to set your shot up. The first task is to find a suitable view point. Fireworks are great near water where you can capture magnificent reflections. Usually fireworks start when there is no light in the sky at all but if you can capture some sky light it will improve your shot. Look around for other lights that can aid the photograph. Find trees or people as foreground silhouettes. You will need to estimate how high the fireworks will go and determine how wide of a shot to use. This needs to be done well before the show begins.

You can use your self timer set to 2 seconds if you do not have a remote control cable however, it will be difficult to time the fireworks. I used my self timer in the photo to the right and got lucky.

Try to use the fireworks as a backdrop to a photo like the one on the next page.

Warwick Firemen's Carnival
Canon 7D - 18mm, 6s @ f16

Facing Page: Warwick Firemen's Festival
Canon 7D, 50mm, 4 seconds @ f22, ISO 400

Prepare in advance

• Set your camera to full manual. You want to control the shutter speed and aperture yourself. Don't let the camera do this.

• *ISO*: Use a low ISO for a clean photo, try 100 to 400. White balance to tungsten.

• *Shutter speed*: Use a shutter speed long enough to capture the trails of light. Try 2 seconds for short trails and 6 seconds for long trails. Or shoot in Bulb mode. Only use bulb if you have a remote control for your camera. Use it to hold the shutter open manually until you get the entire burst.

• *Aperture*: The aperture is crucial but you must experiment before you know what is the best. Too large and your colors will wash out and it will be hard to get a good focus. Too small and they won't show up. Start with f8 to f16.

• Set your focus to manual. It will take time for the camera to automatically focus on the fireworks and you may miss the moment. It will be best to set this manually and leave it alone.

• Make sure your flash is turned off. Or try a shot with slow sync flash if you want to expose the foreground with fireworks in the background.

• If possible, shoot upwind so the smoke is being blown away from you or you may get smoky shots. If there is no wind the first shots will be your best clearest. Sometimes smoke lit up from the busts can be interesting as well.

Multiple Exposures

Another technique is to set your camera to record multiple exposures in one. If your camera does not support this mode there is an easy manual work around.

Bring a dark object with you such as a black piece of cardboard or cloth. Set your camera to the BULB setting and lock your remote to open the shutter. Next hold the cardboard in front of the lens so that no light gets through. If it is night this will be no problem. You can hold the object a couple inches in front of the lens and no light will get in. Now all you have to do is pull the cardboard away each time a rocket is launched and explodes, then cover the lens until the next one launches.

This will give you multiple explosions on one image. A word of caution. If the fireworks are exploding in the same area you will continue to expose each burst over the next and all you will get for an image is a big white blob. The more color that is added the whiter the image will get as seen in this image. I find that the best photos contain two or three bursts at different levels but go ahead and experiment.

Photo taken from roadside near Montgomery along route 416
Canon 7D, 30mm, 1.5 seconds @ f32, ISO 100, EV +0.3, white balance: shade

You've already learned how to white balance your camera so that what is supposed to be white is actually white. Now let me tell you about white unbalance. When do you want white not to be white? To answer that question, imagine you're walking on a beach in the middle of the day and you're wearing a white shirt. Someone takes your picture. What color should your shirt be in the picture? White! Now imagine you come back in the evening wearing the same shirt and there is a beautiful sunset with an orange glow. Someone takes your picture again. What color should your shirt be? It should be orange. But your camera's automatic white balance (AWB) will try it's best to rid the photo of the orange glow thus eliminating much of the color from the sunset.

If it is your intention is to keep the color cast in the photo you must set your white balance to the lighting behind what ever is making the color cast. For example, the sun shining through the atmosphere at a low angle is creating the red/orange glow. So set your camera to sun. To exaggerate the orange glow of a sunset try the shade white balance.

I was once in an elementary school classroom where they created the sensation of being under water. They covered the fluorescent lights with blue cellophane and the children cutout and decorated fish which they hung from the ceiling. The cellophane cast a blue light around the room. To photograph this scene while keeping the blue color cast you would have to set your white balance to fluorescent, the light source behind the filter.

Sam's Point Preserve
Canon 20D, 50mm, 1/160 @f8, ISO 400, EV. -0.7, saturation +1

If you are shooting directly into the sun you will find that the camera's light meter will get confused and under expose the photo such as in the example on the facing page. In most cases this provides the desired effect with a silhouetted foreground. However, if the sun is not in your photograph and your intention is to capture the orange glow from the sun such as the above photo then you have some camera settings to manipulate. Your camera will try to make everything look like a bright sunny day thus over-exposing the photograph. When a photograph is over exposed, the color will be washed out. To fix this, not only should you choose a sunny, cloudy or shade white balance manually, you should also under expose the image slightly. By underexposing this image the orange glow is evident on the rocks and the people's faces. Use exposure compensation to under expose your photographs.

If you remember the lesson about white balance, you will remember that when selecting a white balance setting that is cooler than the light you are photographing the result is an over compensated warmth in your photograph. Look at the scale below. If your white balance is set to shade then anything white in the shade will look white. But if you leave your camera on this setting and take photos in the sun, everything white will look orange. This means that your sunset photos will have even more of an orange tint to them.

Warmer   Cooler

Bashakill, Wurtsboro, sundown.
Canon 7D, 1s @ f22 ISO 100, 28mm, white balance: daylight
EV: -1.3, saturation: +3

BLUE LIGHT HOUR

Church Park, Goshen

Blue Hour refers to the time after the sun goes below the horizon and the sky goes into deep blue for a while just before it gets dark. This is the best time to take night photos, especially of Christmas Lights. At this time you will achieve those deep blue skies in your photos. The "Blue Hour" does not last for an entire hour as the name suggests. You only have about 15 minutes to capture this beautiful lighting. So be ready before the sun goes down, then wait.

As always, when there is low light you will have to use a tripod. Use a small aperture to keep both close up and distant objects in focus. Notice that I used f22 on the top photo. Remember, large numbers mean small aperture sizes. Use a large aperture to blur backgrounds such as the photo on the next page. In this photo I used f4.5 to blur the tree lights in the background.

Facing page: Orange County Arboretum, Montgomery
Canon 7D, 36mm, 1/12 @f4.5 ISO 400, Color Saturation +3

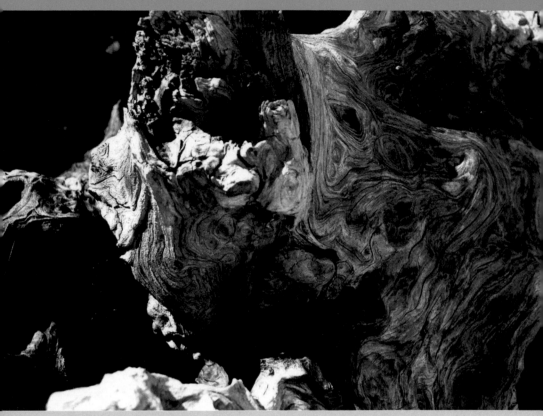

Giant Redwood Tree Roots shipped from California on private property in Ulster County
Canon 7D, 50mm, 1/160 @ f8, ISO 100

Private Property

At first I wasn't sure if it would be appropriate to include photo locations on private land but after some careful consideration I decided it was worth the risk. After all, there is absolutely no problem with contacting the owner and asking permission. There are some wonderful photography opportunities on private land throughout the Mid-Hudson Valley. Just be sure to contact the owner or the local police department before wandering in.

Photography and the Law

There is a lot of misinformation out there regarding taking public photographs especially of people. I am not an attorney so be advised that none of what is written here should be used as legal advice. However, as a general matter, you do not need any permission to take photographs of people or buildings in a public place. If you are permitted to view it with your naked eye you are permitted to record it with your camera.

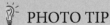
PHOTO TIP

I find it is best to call before attempting to photograph after hours or on questionable property. Call the local police to inform them if you plan on staying at a public park after dusk. Most of the time people are ecstatic to help you out and to show off their treasures. You may be invited to a special location you never knew existed. Try asking before photographing. You'll be surprised.

Gear hub of an old water wheel on private property in Monroe
Canon 7D, 50mm, 1/4s @ f5.6, ISO 100

Photo Releases

A written release is required to prevent anyone from suing for a share of gains acquired from commercial use of their image.

If you sell your work on a large scale or use it in a commercial manner then you need to acquire a written release.

Photography in a private place

When you are in a private place such as a store or museum your "rights" as a photographer can be limited and you will have to follow their rules. If their rule is no photography then you cannot take pictures.

Pools of blue-green water above Nevele Falls in Ellenville accessed across private property
Canon 7D, 50mm, 4 seconds @ f22, ISO 100

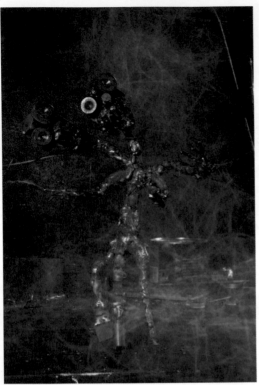

Photography in a public location

Any public display can be photographed without permission as long as the intention is for personal use. Even photographing kids on the street is not an illegal activity. But like anything else, the law recognizes reasonableness and notions of common sense. Following someone around taking numerous photographs will attract the attention of the law and you will have to answer for your actions. Just because someone or something is within public access does not give you the right to be abusive or obsessive.

Most public parks close at dusk to prevent anybody from staying after dark to engage in illegal activity. Photography is not one of them although we all have to obey the same rules. I've been locked inside park gates and have had people call the police about my unusual activities so I now notify the local police department if I ever intend to stay out late. In every instance the police were very accommodating and I thank them sincerely.

Barzal Metal Studios - Metal Sculptures created by Zac Shavrick
Canon 7D, 24mm, 1/200 @f22 ISO 400

Frozen Water Tower on private land near Rio Reservoir, Sullivan County
Canon 7D, 36mm, 1/400sec, f11, ISO 400 HDR

Professional photography not allowed

I find it curious that some people actually think taking a good photograph is against the law. Unless you are on private property, nobody can tell you that you can't take pictures, professional or amateur. Things change quickly though when you start hauling in tripods and other equipment. Also you may be limited to how you use the photographs. When someone writes a rule that professional photography is not allowed it means they don't want photos of their property being placed on post cards, calendars, billboards and other commercial venues, not that they don't want you to take a great picture for your wall. But when ill-informed staff see a camera that looks like something they could never under-stand how to use they pull that rule out of the back of their minds and slam it down on you. When you try to convince them that you are just an amateur willing to drop a little cash on a good camera and tripod they slam you with the "tripping hazard" rule. I've never seen a tripod resist giving way to someone's wayward foot. The end result never ends with the pedestrian falling to the ground but always the camera tumbling down with an expensive crash. Photographers are very careful to avoid that. I was recently reminded how narrow minded people can be when I visited the Boscobel House in Garrison where I was asked to pay a $250 professional photographer's fee or leave the property. They stood there with smug looks on their faces watching me as I packed up my gear as if they had just intercepted a menace who might be spray painting graffiti or digging up flowers from their garden. I was escorted to my car. I guess they were afraid I might sneak back in and do the unthinkable, take a good picture. What are they going to do when cell phones can take good pictures? Have everybody check their phones at the door? So I don't have a picture of their house hanging on my wall. I can live with that. Unfortunately it's *their* rule on *their* property and no matter how inconvenient, we have to obey.

Frozen Katrina Falls near Wolf Lake in the Neversink Unique Area
Canon 20D, 38mm, 1/160 @f8 ISO 100

Waterfalls are best in the spring when the ground is saturated with water from snow melt and April showers. Winter scenes of ice covered falls such as Katrina Falls in January (above) are just as breath taking.

There has been some debate about the best way to photograph waterfalls: slow shutter speeds for a silky water effect or fast shutter speed to freeze water droplets. There is no wrong way. It's a matter of personal preference. Personally, I prefer the silky water but I have seen plenty of photos of frozen water droplets that I liked.

PHOTO TIP

If you are using your camera on a tripod with slow shutter speeds, the simple act of pushing down the shutter release button will make the camera move a little causing camera movement blur in your photograph. Using a remote control will prevent this from happening. If you do not have a remote control try setting your shutter mode to 2 second timer. The camera will not take the photo until two seconds have passed after pressing the shutter release. This gives you time to move your hands away from the camera.

Facing page: Fitzgerald Falls along the Appalachian Trail in Monroe off Lakes Road.
Canon 7D, 29mm, 1.3s @f10 ISO 100, Color Saturation +3, contrast +1

You often have to hike a bit to find the good falls but most are easily accessible and not far from a parking area. You can drive right up to the man-made falls or dams such as Croton Dam near Peekskill. But if you don't mind going for a little walk, natural water falls are fun to photograph.

Photographing Silky Water

By now you probably realize that if you don't use a tripod you may want to start trying it out. As I mentioned earlier, there are two ways to photograph waterfalls. By far, the most popular is the silky water effect. To accomplish this you must use a fairly slow shutter speed, about 1/2 a second give or take. Faster for less silk, slower for more. These speeds are too slow to hand hold your camera so a tripod is needed.

To obtain the silky water effect turn your ISO as low as it can go. Make sure it is not set to automatic. Next, place your camera in shutter priority mode and select the shutter speed you wish to use. Let the camera decide on the aperture value.

Croton Dam at Croton Gorge Park near Peekskill
Canon 7D, 36mm, 1/25 @f22 ISO 100, Color
Saturation +3

Stony Kill Falls, Wawarsing
Canon 7D, 55mm, 1/200sec @f5.6 ISO 100

Facing page: Split Rock, Mohonk Preserve
Canon 7D, 36mm, 2.5s @f32 ISO 100

Stone Church, Dover Plains
Canon 7D, 32mm, 1/2s @f13 ISO 100

If your are out on a bright sunny day there may be too much light. On a bright day your camera may not be able to achieve a slow enough shutter speed. Even if you turn the ISO all the way down and close the aperture all the way down you still may not get shutter speeds under 1/100th of a second. There is only one option at this point. You must add a neutral density filter to your equipment bag. A neutral density filter will reduce the amount of light coming into the camera thus slowing down your shutter speed. If a neutral density filter is not available, try coming back in the evening as the sun is going down or return on day with heavy cloud cover.

Awosting Falls, Minnewaska State Park
Canon 20D, 55mm, 1/4s @f29 ISO 100

Freezing water droplets in mid air
I don't mean winter time photos like the one two pages back . If you use a fast shutter speed such as 1/1000 of a second your camera will capture the water drops crystal clear as they fall thus freezing them in time. This can be equally as rewarding as the silky photos where the water droplets are blurred as they fall due to the slower shutter speed. You will need a lot of light for this project. This is especially intriguing when water is splashing up like an ocean wave hitting the rocks. Experiment and have fun.

Indian Brook Falls in Cold Spring, NY
Canon 7D, 55mm, 1s @f16 ISO 100

Waterfalls and Dams of the Hudson Valley:

Location	Town	County	Page
Algonquin Park	Newburgh	Orange Count	
Awosting Falls, Minnewaska Preserve	Shawangunk	Ulster County	101
Bard College	Red Hook	Dutchess County	
Croton Dam	Croton	Westchester County	99
Falling Waters Preserve	Glasco	Ulster County	
Fitzgerald Falls	Monroe	Putnam County	97
Indian Brook Falls	Cold Spring	Putnam County	101
Katrina Falls	Cuddebackville	Sullivan County	96, 103
Nevele Falls	Ellenville	Ulster County	
Peters Kill Falls & Ruins	Shawangunk	Ulster County	
Split Rock, Mohonk Preserve	Shawangunk	Ulster County	98
Stone Church	Dover Plains	Dutchess County	100
Stony Kill Falls	Wawarsing	Ulster County	99
Verkeerder Falls, Sam's Point	Shawangunk	Ulster County	102
West Point Foundry Preserve	Cold Spring	Putnam County	

Verkeerder Falls, Sam's Point,

Facing page: Katrina Falls, Neversink Unique Area Canon 20D, 20mm, 1/2sec @ f14.0, ISO 100

CREATING MOOD

Brick Church Cemetery, Montgomery
Canon 7D, 50mm, 1/160 @f14 ISO 100, EV. -2.3

Believe it or not, your camera has the power to change the time of day. This photo looks like it was taken at night during a full moon. In fact, it was taken at noon during a bright sunny day with no clouds in the sky. I used a few simple techniques to achieve my midnight mood.

First- If your camera has the Kelvin option, select the lowest Kelvin temperature your camera is capable of. If it does not support Kelvin then choose Tungsten from the white balance presets. Tungsten is 3200 degrees Kelvin, very low on the scale.

Next- under expose the image about 2 stops. Use your exposure compensation adjustment (AV) and point it to -2 on the scale.

Shoot away and your photos will look like they are taken at night.

Picture Style	(). ().&.()
A Auto	3 , 0 , 0 , 0
S Standard	3 , 0 , 0 , 0
P Portrait	2 , 0 , 0 , 0
L Landscape	4 , 0 , 0 , 0
N Neutral	0 , 0 , 0 , 0
F Faithful	0 , 0 , 0 , 0
INFO Detail set.	SET OK

Now we'll make daytime out of the night. The photo below was taken after the sun went down. It was dark but not completely dark. After all, you need some light to take a photo. It doesn't have to be much but you can't take a photograph if there is no light at all.

First - Get out your tripod. In low light your shutter speed will be too slow to hand hold your camera so a tripod is a must.

Next - Use Picture Styles or Picture Control to boost the color saturation. I used +3 in the photo below. You will often lose contrast when over exposing a photo so boost the contrast up a little as well. I used +2. Picture styles can be found in your camera's menu.

Finally - Over expose the photo a little bit using the exposure compensation adjustment similar to what was done on the previous page but in the plus direction.

You're ready to shoot. It may take a few practice shots and tweaking to get it right but these settings are a good place to start. Don't forget to set your camera back to normal when you are finished.

Taken at the top of Perkin's Memorial Drive at Bear Mountain
Canon 7D, 36mm, 1/2 @f4.5 ISO 200, AV +1, Color Saturation +3, Contrast +2

Hillside Cemetery, Middletown
Canon 7D, 50mm, 30s @ f32, ISO 100, EV. +0.3, white balance: tungsten

Some may think it is morbid but cemeteries can be a lot of fun for a photographer, especially in the autumn or winter. Weathered monuments and ancient trees create eerie photographs. I was always intrigued by special effects photography with superimposed or semitransparent images. What better place to experiment with this than a cemetery. There are literally hundreds of old cemeteries around the Hudson Valley. Some online resources include www.rootsweb.ancestry.com and find. mapmuse.com/map/cemeteries. Everybody seems to know where an old cemetery is nearby their home town.

 PHOTO TIP

To make ghosts in your photos, visit the cemetery just before it gets dark. Place your camera on a tripod and use shutter priority mode to force a long exposure (about 10-20 seconds). Have your subject stand still for half the exposure then quickly walk out of the photo. The result will be a semi transparent image of a person.

If there is too much light to get a long exposure try adjusting the ISO as low as it will go and closing your aperture all the way down. If that still doesn't work you'll have to wait until it gets a little darker or use a neutral density filter.

Facing Page: Brick Church Cemetery, Montgomery
Canon 7D, 50mm, 1/100 @ f 5.6, ISO 1600, contrast +2, saturation +3

Maple leaf adrift in Trout Brook near Fitzgerald Falls along the Appalachian Trail in Monroe
Canon 7D, 138mm, 1/8 @ f5.6, ISO 200, saturation +2, contrast +2

In 2002 New York's Governor George Pataki dedicated a long suspension foot bridge spanning Popolopen Creek connecting Fort Montgomery and Fort Clinton. The twin forts were a strategic stronghold during the American Revolutionary war. Fierce battles were fought here for control over the Hudson River. The forts were finally destroyed by the British on October 6, 1777.

Today the bridge provides pedestrians access to the Bear Mountain Trail Side Zoo from the Fort Montgomery Museum and archeological site. Parking is available at the Fort Montgomery Visitor Center off 9W. There are great views of the Bear Mountain Bridge from the walkway. It is a great place to capture images of autumn.

Fort Montgomery State Historic Site is a genuine vestige of our nation's struggle for independence.

Facing Page: Popolopen Creek Suspension Foot Bridge
Canon 7D, 50mm, 1/100 @ f16, ISO 100, saturation +3

Autumn is an exhilarating time to take photographs. There are a few things you should know before donning your camera and heading out the door.

First and foremost, get a circular polarizer filter. A Polarizer screws on to the front of your camera lens and filters unpolarized light. As light is reflected off your subject it is scattered in different directions randomly. If the surface is reflective most of the light rays are bounced back without being scattered. The polarizer filter can be rotated to filter out these reflecting rays of light so that the true color of the object is seen. It is often used to remove glare from water or glass but it also helps brighten up the color in your photographs. It is especially useful when photographing fall foliage.

Next, switch off automatic white balance. Choose a preset or learn how to custom white balance your camera. When photographing lots of warm color the automatic setting will become confused and make the picture unrealistically cold. You will loose some of those warm colors. By forcing a white balance setting the camera will keep the warmth of those fall colors.

Watch for over exposures. Over exposing your photo will wash out the colors. Use the exposure compensation setting (AV) to under expose a little.

Finally, use picture control to bring up the color saturation a bit. Your fall leaves will pop!

Roadside stand in Ulster County
Canon 7D, 32mm, 1/25s @ f 4.5, ISO 400

Facing page: Indian Brook, Cold Spring
Canon 7D, 30mm, 1/10sec @ f4.0, ISO 100

Rule of Thirds

One rule every photographer should understand is the rule of thirds. This rule simply says not to place your subject right in the center of your photograph. Most photographs are more interesting when your main subject is off to one side. Imagine a tick-tack-toe board superimposed over your photograph. Now position your subject where the lines cross. Refer to the photo of the butterfly at the top of the facing page. If you have a long subject such as a lake horizon then place it over one of the third lines. It's that simple. It won't work with every photograph but you'll be amazed at what it can do to improve most shots. Some cameras have a grid built in. You can enable it through your camera's menu or the display button on the back of your camera.

Balance

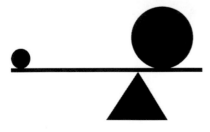

Learning how to balance your photographs will help improve your images. We already learned that it is important to move your subject from the center of the photograph using the rule of thirds. Now we have to learn what to do with the rest of the space. You must use this space to balance your photograph.

In this photograph, we used the stones to help balance the image. Imagine two children on a see saw or teeter totter. If one child is heavier than the other, the equipment will not function. To create balance, the pivot point needs to move closer to the heavier child. This same rule applies to photography. Notice how this technique was used in the above photograph. The small stones on the left help to balance the image of the girl on the right.

Golden Mean

The rule of thirds is actually derived from the Golden Mean or the Golden Ratio. The golden mean being a more elaborate version of the rule of thirds. It is actually a mathematical ratio. This ratio seems to pop up naturally all around us. It has been described as perfect beauty. Objects that have the golden ratio as their physical makeup appear to be beautiful. To use the golden ratio in your photographs place the most intricate detailed part of the image at the center of the curve and work less and less detail towards the opposite end.

Fun with steel wool on the rail trail trestle in New Paltz
Canon 7D, 12s @ f4.6, ISO 400

Hudson Valley Rail Trails

Dutchess Rail Trail
    from Poughkeepsie to Hopewell
        Junction
    www.dutchessrailtrail.com

Heritage Trail: 12.4 miles (paved)
    from Goshen to Monroe

Putnam County Trailway: 12 miles
    Somers to Brewster Heights
    www.traillink.com/trail/putnam-trailway.aspx

Walden - Wallkill Rail Trail: 3.22 miles (paved)
    from Walden to Wallkill
    www.traillink.com/trail/shawangunk-walden-and-wallkill-rail-trail.aspx

Walkway over the Hudson: 1.28 miles (paved)

Wallkill Valley Rail Trail: 23.7 miles
    from Gardiner to Kingston
    www.traillink.com/trail/wallkill-valley-rail-trail.aspx

Rail Trails

In the mid 1960's as railroads became defunct people started using the abandoned gravel roadbeds as trails. Quietly and gradually the idea spread from the midwest out to each coast. The idea was a good one and people liked it thus "Rails-to-Trails" was born. There are now over 15,000 miles of rail-trails across the US.

Whether you hike, bike, run, roller blade or walk, bring your camera along and get some nice shots.

Many of the rail trails have been paved but many are still dirt trails like the Heritage Trail North of Goshen (right). Plans are to complete the trail to Middletown. Many Trestles have been converted to walking bridges, the Walkway Over the Hudson being one of the more famous but others such as the Wallkill Rail Trestle in Rosendale (below) have also been converted. More and more rails have turned to trails every year. Grab your camera and hop on your bike. Let's go for a ride.

Wallkill Rail Trail across the Rosendale Train Trestle
Canon 7D, 18mm, 1/200 @ f3.5, ISO 100

HISTOGRAM

There are two types of people. Those who, as a child, separated their M&Ms by color before eating them and those who just ate them without any organization at all. I was a sorter. Perhaps that is why I can understand histograms well. A histogram is simply shades of brightness sorted in columns starting from the darkest (shadows) on the left and continuing to the lightest (highlights) on the right.

All images are composed of tiny dots or pixels which show up as square when zoomed in very close on the computer. When I was in grade school my art teacher gave the class an assignment to draw a photo by simply placing dots on the paper. Up close the picture I drew didn't have much definition until you stepped away and looked at it from a distance. From further away the dots appeared to be closer together and smaller thus increasing the resolution which in turn, made the drawing look more like the paddle steam boat I had envisioned. The same goes for digital photographs. They are composed of millions of tiny dots. The histogram takes every one of the dots and separates them by shades from black to white. Very similar to the way I used to separate my M&Ms by color. So image yourself creating an image with all those colored M&Ms. And after completing it you sort those M&Ms in columns from darkest to lightest colors. That is what a histogram is.

To help us envision this we are going to desaturate the image of the butterfly below and zoom in close to examine a 36 pixel section on the next page.

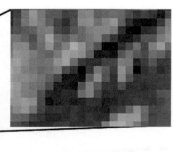

Since a full image has millions of pixels it would be difficult to explain how a histogram works unless I simplify it. In the diagram below on the right side is a very small section of the butterfly image containing only 36 pixels. On the left is a simple histogram of the pixels found in that small portion of the image. You can see that there are eight pixels that are very dark, seven that are a little less dark, continuing through the levels until we reach four that are white. This is how pixels are displayed in a histogram.

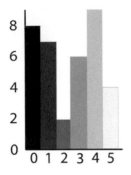

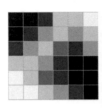

Rondout Creek, Rosendale from Trestle
Canon 7D, 22mm, 1/80sec @ f14, ISO 100

Now imagine this with millions of pixels. On the right we have a full image with sky, clouds, water and trees. Below you can see the full histogram of that image. The trees are dark so those pixels are counted on the left side. The clouds are light so those pixels are counted on the right side.

Using the histogram we can determine if the picture is exposed properly. When you see pixels stacking up on the left or right side, there is probably an exposure problem.

The picture on the left is under exposed and the picture on the right is over exposed. You can see this clearly in the images. You can also see it clearly in their respective histograms below the images. Notice the collection of increasing black pixels climbing on the left of the first histogram and the increasing white pixels climbing on the right of the second histogram. Compare these histograms to the properly exposed histogram on the previous page. So why do you need a histogram to show you what you can clearly see in the image? Because not every, in fact most improper exposures are not so easy to see by looking at the LCD screen on the back of the camera. These things usually are not noticed until you get home and view them on a larger computer monitor when it is too late. What do I mean too late? Exposure can be easily corrected in photo editing software right? Exposures can be corrected, however lost detail is lost forever.

Detail

That white cloud isn't all pure white. If it was, it would just be a white blob. It is not a white blob. There are many shades of white in it. That is how we see the detail, because it is not just one solid shade of white. If that cloud is over exposed it becomes one shade of white, a big white blob. The histogram shows that the camera did not capture the various shades. When the image is darkened with software to correct the exposure you will then have a gray blob still without detail. If you want a good exposure. Look at the histogram.

Town Parks

A great place to find nice photography is at your local town park. You never know what interesting subjects will turn up in a town park. Subjects such as old air craft, railroad cars, old buildings and bridges. Every town has a park. Bring your camera and a lunch and spend the day hunting for photographs. Find your park's website for activities and events. Local parks are a great resource for photography.

If you've been to your own park too often and it now seems too mundane to photograph then it's time to visit your neighboring towns. There are too many to list here.

Stanley Deming Park, Warwick, NY
Canon 7D, 124s @ f11

Canon 7D, 1/80s @ f5.6, ISO 100

⚪PHOTO TIP

There are a few ways to achieve great cloud pictures. One way is to use a polarizer filter. Every photographer should have one in his camera bag. Polarizers help to keep stray light from washing out the bright areas of your photographs. They also bring out the blue in the sky. Another method is to use a graduated neutral density filter. These filters darken the sky to prevent over exposure. Yet another option is to shoot in the evening as the sky is getting dark and use flash to brighten up your foreground. You can also use HDR software to blend images of various exposures. All these methods work great.

Facing Page: Old tower, Salesian Park, Goshen, NY.
Canon 20D, 70mm, 1/250 @ f5.6, ISO 100

State and National Parks

A great resource for state parks along the Hudson River is Scenic Hudson: www.sce-nichudson.org. Here you will find a list of about 35 state parks with maps, photos and directions. It's a great place to start if you're looking for photographic places to visit in the Hudson Valley.

I've been very fortunate to have the opportunity to visit many of these parks including Poet's Walk, Foundry Dock Park, Franny Reese State Park, Long Dock Park, Walkway Over the Hudson, West Point Foundry Preserve and more.

Poet's Walk, Red Hook
Canon 7D, 1/30sec @ f8

Hudson Valley Parks

Every place listed in this book is a park of sorts but these are the places with the word "Park" actually in the name.

Location	Town	County
Algonquin Park	Newburgh	Orange County
Charles Rider Park	Kingston	Ulster County
Church Park	Goshen	Orange County, pg 57
Clarence Fahnestock State Park	Hopewell Junctioni	Putnam County
Croton Point Park	Croton	Westchester County, pg 5
Dater Mountain Natural Park	Sloatsburg	Rockland County
Dockside Park	Cold Spring	Putnam County, pg 6
Elk Brox Memorial Park	Port Jervis	Orange County, pg 75
Foundry Dock Park	Cold Spring	Putnam County
Franny Reese State Park	Highland	Ulster County, pg 48
Highland Lakes State Park	Scotchtown	Orange County
Highland Landing Park	Highland	Ulster County
Huckleberry Ridge State Park	Port Jervis	Orange County
Hudson Highland Gateway Park	Cortlandt	Westchester County
Kaal Rock Park	Esopus	Ulster County
Long Dock Park	Beacon	Dutchess County, pg 4
Madam Brett Park	Beacon	Dutchess County
Mount Beacon Park	Beacon	Dutchess County
Peach Hill Park	Poughkeepsie	Dutchess County
Perrine's Bridge Park	Esopus-Rosendale	Ulster County, pg 47, 61
Quiet Cove Park	Poughkeepsie	Dutchess County
Reese Park	Wappingers	Dutchess County
Robert E Post Memorial Park	Kingston	Ulster County
Salesian Park	Goshen	Orange County
Sleightsburgh Park	Esopus	Ulster County
Stony Point State Park	Stony Point	Rockland County, pg 123
Waryas Park	Poughkeepsie	Dutchess County
Winding Hills Park	Montgomery	Orange County

Stony Point State Park
Canon 7D, 75mm, 1/60sec @ f22 ISO 100

💡 PHOTO TIP

Don't put your camera away on a gloomy day. The flat lighting and interesting cloud formations can create mood in your photographs not to mention the sheen from wet ground and leaves. Some of my favorite photos were taken when the sun wasn't showing itself in the sky. Be wary of your camera getting wet if you don't have one that's water resistant. Bring an umbrella if you have to but try to keep that shutter snapping.

Goose Pond Mountain State Park, Monroe
Canon 7D, 18mm, 1/125sec, f6.3, ISO 100

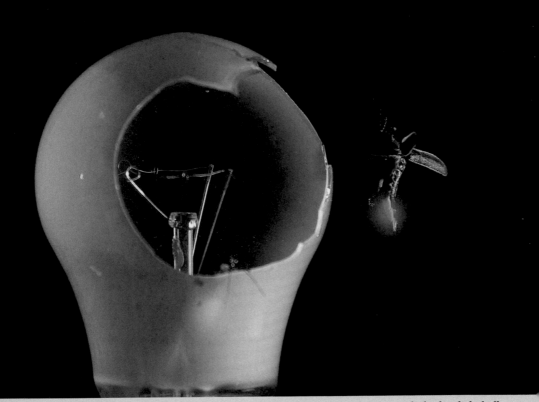

Off camera remote flash was used to capture this lightning bug flying out of a broken light bulb.
Photo by Jeff Montanye and Joseph Kuzmiak - Canon 7D, 120mm, 1/25s @ f5.6, ISO 100, flash -1

Flash is the most misused part of the camera. Unless you are a miner and are used to having a light attached to your head all day, the most unnatural way to light your subject is from the same angle or perspective you are viewing the subject. Unfortunately there really isn't a better place to put the flash on a camera. The best option your flash has is the off button. But it just isn't practical to think you will never use your flash. If you must use flash it is best to use an external bounce flash with remote capabilities. However, many times you have to resort to the built in flash on your camera. The next few pages will show you the best ways to use this flash and still have a good photo.

Here are some of the problems we have to overcome with our flash:
1) Foreground objects are bright while background objects are very dark
2) Mixed lighting temperatures, room lights are yellow
3) Washed out foreground
4) Dark shadow around your subject
5) Flat image without good shadow details
6) Blinking, squinting, red eye

This is a typical birthday party snapshot. The first mistake happens when you don't pay attention to everything in your photo. Background junk clutters the photo. The photo is taken while standing, looking down at the subject. It is best to get eye-level with your subject. The subject looks uncomfortable and posed dead center. Flash is turned on which causes an undesirable dark shadow around the subject. A bright sunbeam is over-exposing the hair. We can improve this shot in just a few steps.

The first thing I did was ask the subject to move about two feet to her left. Then I took two steps to my left and got on my knee. There was a white sweater flung over the back of a chair next to me. I asked my brother-in-law to hold it in the sunbeam which reflected the light back at the subject. Finally I turned off the flash. The difference was like night and day!

Shutters

Just like film, your Digital SLR camera's CCD chip is sensitive to light all the time. The tiny light collecting cells are always active therefore it is unable to control the exposure without blocking the light with a mechanical shutter. The shutter is a curtain that blocks light from exposing the CCD chip until the shutter release button is pushed. At that time the shutter moves out of the way so that light can expose the CCD chip for a pre-programmed amount of time. These shutters have been used in cameras going way back to the earliest models. Not all digital cameras have shutters. Most compact cameras can turn the CCD chip on and off to control the exposure instead of blocking it with a shutter. Some have a micro shutter built right into the lens, so small and light that it can move much faster than it's larger DSLR brothers. This works well for a camera without changeable lenses and very small CCD chips but not for the higher quality DSLRs. The way DSLR cameras, lenses and the electronics inside are currently built, the mechanical shutter has multiple benefits over

electronic shutters and to change things now means pretty much throwing away everything we have and starting fresh. Some camera manufacturers are doing this now. The new electronic viewfinder interchangeable lens (EVIL) cameras and mirrorless interchangeable lens cameras (MILC) have hit the market. But these still fall short of the quality and features of true digital single lens reflex (DSLR) cameras.

Flash Sync Speed

Light is fast. One hundred eighty six thousand miles per second fast. There is no camera so fast that it can move faster than the speed of light. If that is the case then why are there limits with flash on our cameras? Turn your camera's built in flash on and look at the shutter speed the camera selected. You probably see 1/60th of a second for a shutter speed. This is the standard flash sync speed. What will happen if you try to choose a shutter speed faster than that? Put your camera in shutter priority mode and increase the shutter speed. It will probably go as far as 1/200th of a second or there about. Today's modern cameras can handle speeds that fast with their built in flash turned on. They won't allow you to use a flash speed beyond the camera's ability. However, older flashes that don't communicate with the camera can be fired using faster shutter speeds. This creates photographs that are only partially exposed. A portion of the image will be black as if something was in front of the camera. Something was in front of the camera, the shutter curtain. That's because the shutter is not fast enough to get out of the way when the flash fires. Light from your flash may travel at the speed of light, but the shutter does not. It takes time for that shutter to move out of the way, hence the reason shutter speed is limited when flash is turned on. It gives the camera time to move the shutter out of the way allowing the entire CCD chip to be exposed in one flash.

Flash Range

Every flash has a maximum useful range. The intensity of the flash when it reaches a subject depends on the flash's power and on how far the light has to travel. The further the subject is from the flash, the less light will reach it and so the less light will be reflected from the subject back toward the camera.

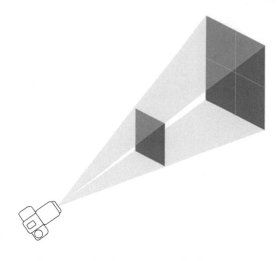

When the flash fires, the beam of light expands as it moves further from the camera so its intensity falls off with distance. Reflected light from your subject continues to disburse as it travels back to the camera. As a result, subjects nearer the flash will be illuminated with a more intense light than subjects farther away. The rate at which the light falls off is described by the inverse square law. The law states that if the distance between the flash and subject is doubled, only one quarter the amount of light will reach the subject because the same amount of light is spread over a larger area. Conversely, when the distance is halved, four times as much light falls on a given area.

Learn the limits of your flash. Take your camera outside and take some evening photos of a tree or car or building with your flash turned on. Walk away and take another shot. Examine the photo each time. This will help you learn how far away from your subject you can be before your flash is not effective. Do not use a subject that is primarily white. White will reflect all the light and give you better results but it will not be an accurate test since most of your subjects will not be white.

Flash on   Flash off

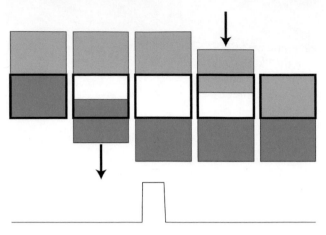

It's Curtains for You

Your camera's shutter is composed of two curtains, each with multiple blades that fold over each other when the shutter is open and fan out when it is closed as seen in the image on the previous page. In the diagram above I've simplified the function of the shutter to two single blade curtains. There are five series of curtain positions displayed above. In each series the dark black square represents the CCD that captures the light to form a photograph. The dark green square represents the first curtain and the light green square represents the second curtain. These curtains are often referred to as front and rear respectively. When the camera is not capturing a photograph the first curtain rests in front of the CCD blocking all light front exposing it as depicted in the first step of the series above. As soon as you press the shutter release the first curtain drops out of the way as you see in the second step. The third step shows the CCD chip completely exposed to light with the first and second curtain out of the way. This is when the flash fires. If it fires at any other time the image will be partially blocked. After the flash has fired the second curtain begins to drop. Once the CCD is completely covered both curtains move back into their original positions.

As the diagram shows, it takes time for the curtains to move across the CCD. This is why there are two curtains. To obtain an even exposure through the entire image, both curtains have to continue in the same direction as they move over the CCD. Engineering this movement is much easier when using two curtains.

High speed flashes allow you to fire the flash at shutter speeds above the flash sync speed. These flashes deliver a series of high speed pulses which continually flash during the exposure.

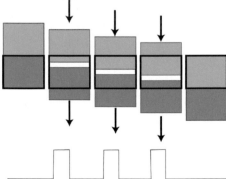

SLOW SYNC

Often the on-camera flash just doesn't perform the way you'd like. Foreground subjects are bright when background subjects are dark. Christmas lights are barely visible tiny spots of light. Subjects are over lighted and shadows are awful. Understanding how your flash works will help you resolve these issues. There are a few good techniques that we will cover here, one of which is Slow Sync.

Flash Modes
Most cameras have two primary flash modes: Manual and TTL (Through The Lens). Lighting results will vary drastically depending on the flash mode you use. The default setting on your camera is TTL so we will start with using that mode. You can check your flash mode in your camera's menu setting under flash Control.

TTL
In order for your camera to calculate the correct exposure automatically it must measure the light bouncing off your subject before it takes the photo. This is easy when you are photographing ambient light because that light is always present. Flash however, is a momentary burst of light at the time you press the shutter release. So how does your camera measure the flash before the flash flashes? TTL flashes emit a pre-flash burst at a reduced power before the shutter opens. This pre-flash lights up your subject and bounces back to your camera and makes the appropriate calculations based on the amount of light bounced back. Once this calculation is made, the camera then opens the shutter and emits a burst of flash precisely calculated to expose your subject properly. This happens so fast that your eye cannot see that there are actually two flashes happening one right after the other.

The Mid-Hudson valley is a great place to explore and photograph. This book only shows a fraction of what can be found along the roads in the counties throughout the river valley. It is my intention to add to this book every year as I continue to hunt for and photograph these wonderful visual treasures. If you have a suggestion for a photographer friendly location or business to add to the guide please contact: Jeff Montanye, PO Box 148, Bullville, NY 10940, 845-361-2029, jmontanye@earthlink.net.

Made in the USA
Middletown, DE
07 July 2022

68649987R00075